Soda Fountain Wisdom

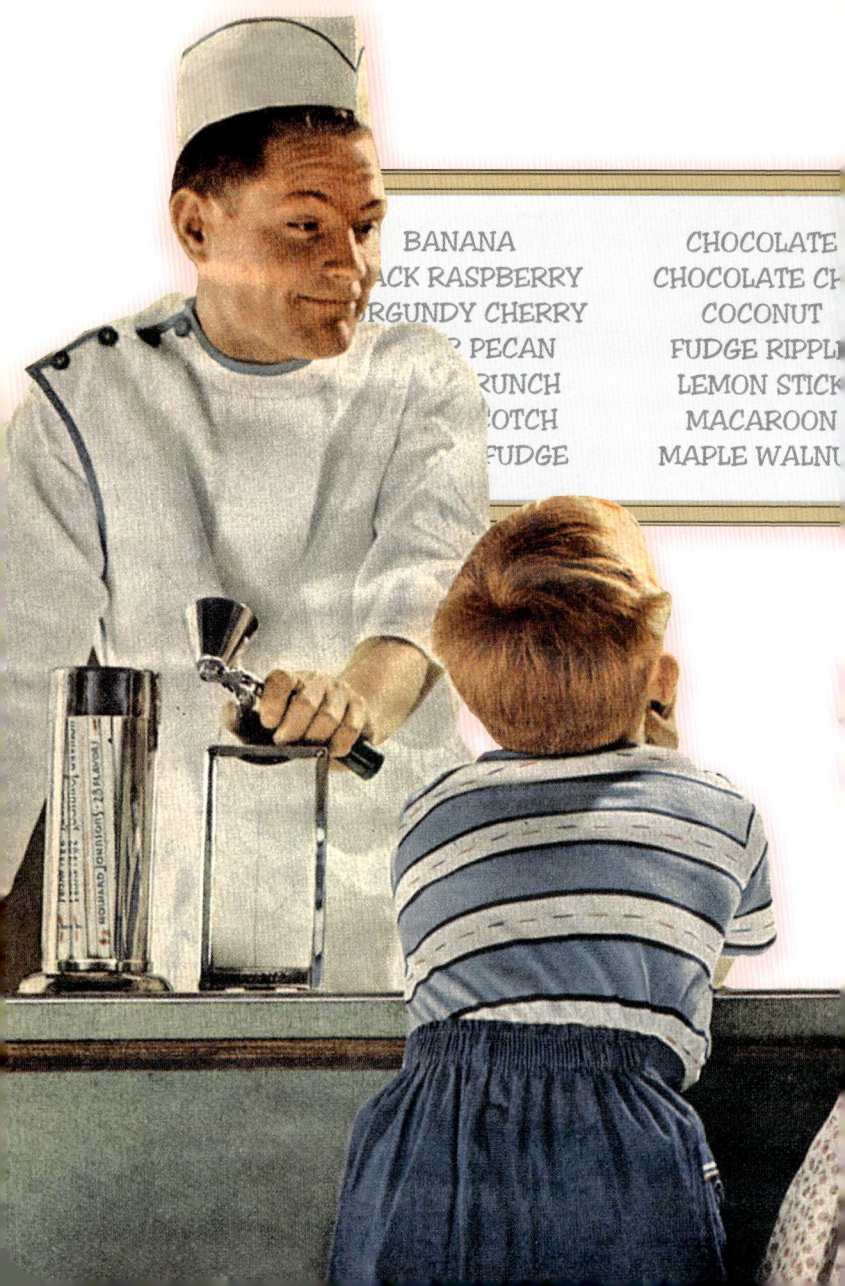

Soda Fountain Wisdom

Wise words from the countertop

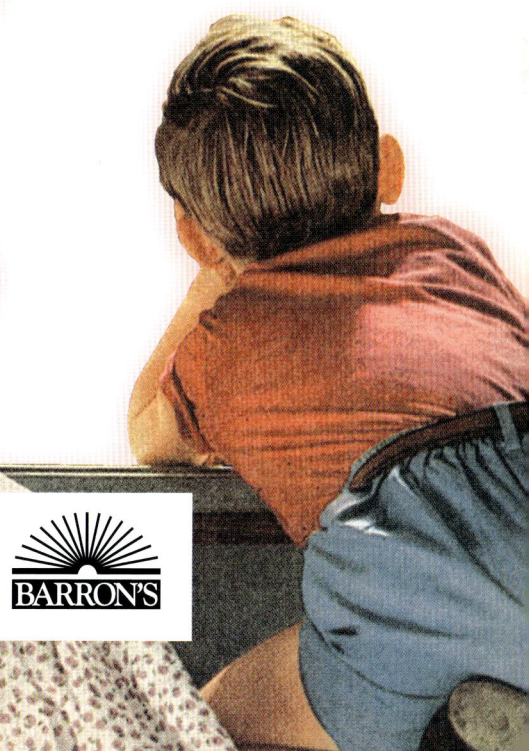

BARRON'S

First edition for North America published in 2004
by Barron's Educational Series, Inc.

Copyright © MQ Publications Ltd 2004

All rights reserved. No part of this book may be reproduced in any form, by photostat, microfilm, xerography, or any others means, or incorporated into any information retrieval system, electronic or mechanical, without the written permission of the copyright owner.

All inquiries should be addressed to:
Barron's Educational Series, Inc.
250 Wireless Boulevard
Hauppauge, NY 11788
http://www.barronseduc.com

International Standard Book No. 0-7641-2726-8
Library of Congress Catalog Card No. 2003109649

Text compilation: Yvonne Deutch
Series Editor: Yvonne Deutch
Design: Lindsey Johns

Printed in China
9 8 7 6 5 4 3 2 1

Chapter 1
MY BLUE HEAVEN

8

Chapter 2
TUTTI FRUTTI

28

Chapter 3
SIPPIN' SODA

60

Chapter 4
TREAT ME NICE

82

Chapter 5
DEVOTED TO YOU

102

Welcome to the soda fountain!

Here, in *Soda Fountain Wisdom*, we evoke memories of a gentler, less hurried time, with visions of shady corners, cool marble countertops, tall swivel stools, and shining soda dispensers. This is where everyone, young and old, was always made welcome—a natural gathering place, where folks exchanged news, views, and an occasional wisecrack thrown in for good measure.

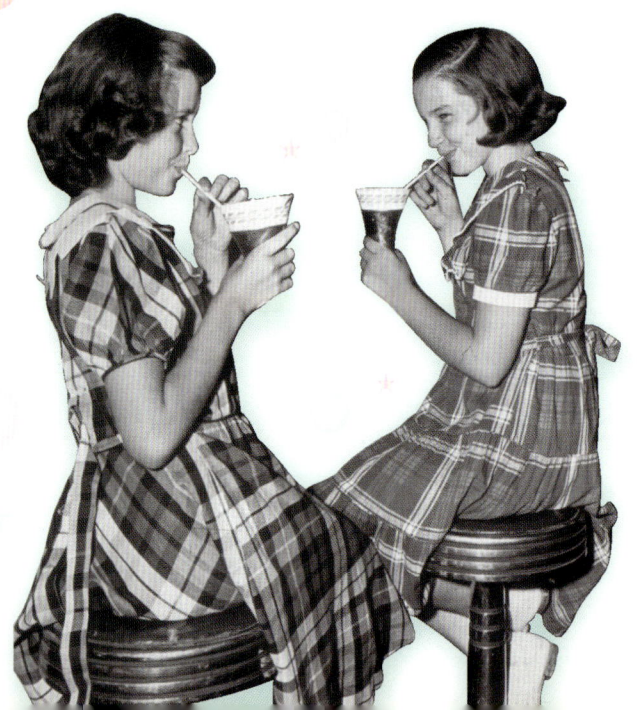

We return to those lost golden days when every town had its neighborhood soda fountain, offering a tempting menu of glorious sweet treats. Who can forget the cool, creamy delight of that first banana split or knickerbocker glory? Or the sheer prettiness of a pink strawberry sundae? All fixed specially for you by the friendly soda jerk, with grace and panache. No wonder so many youngsters wanted to be a soda jerk when they grew up! All that free ice cream! And what about the special drinks? Malts and milk shakes, green rivers, colas and phosphates—with a choice of flavors including lemon, lime, cola, grape, and cherry. In fact, the soda fountain was a distinctive little world, with its own fascinating history and special stories. In *Soda Fountain Wisdom* you'll discover a treasure trove of canny observations, and engaging memories about life shared at the countertop. You can also enjoy historical tidbits, recipes, and unusual snippets of information. Mostly, though, the soda fountain was a place where people found it easy to relax, enjoy an innocent moment of sweetness, and share in the pleasure of neighborly company and kindness.

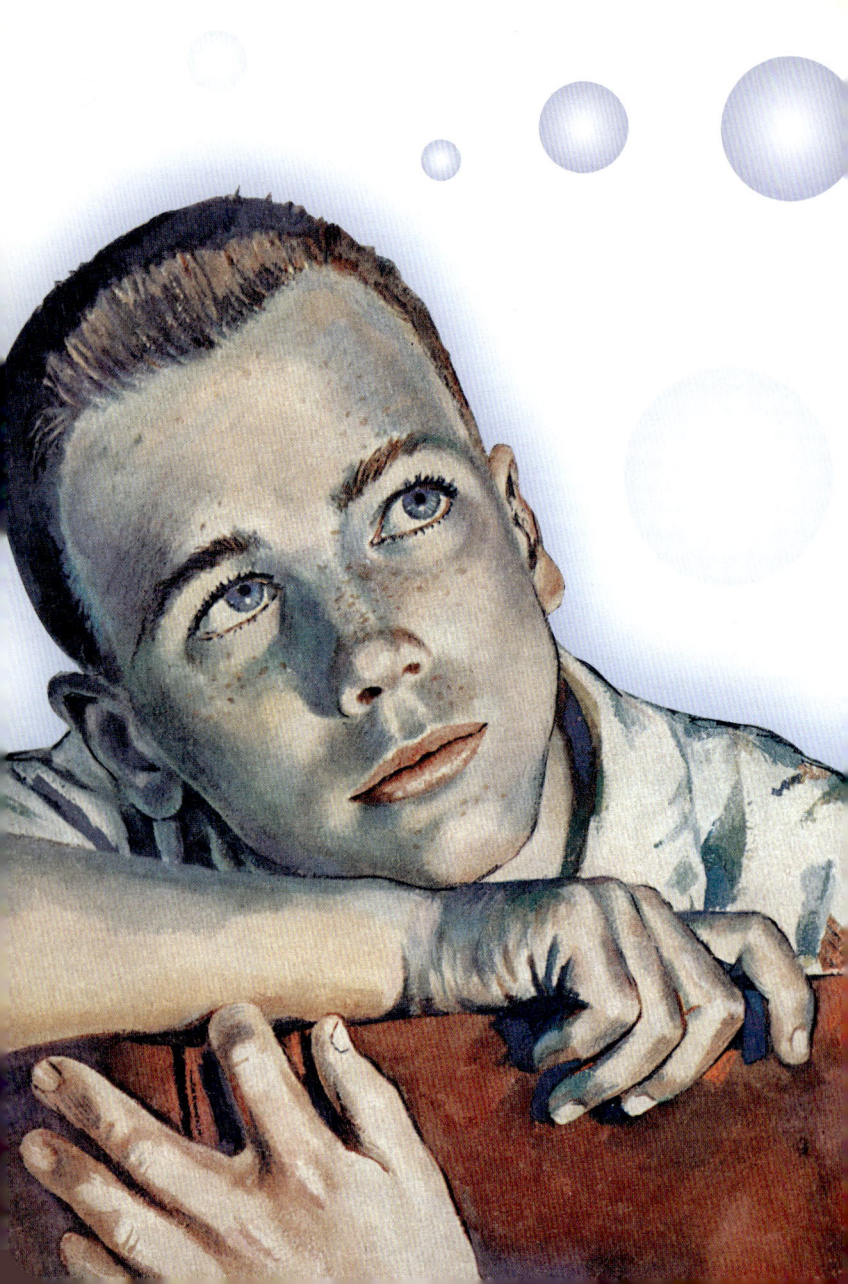

Chapter 1
MY BLUE HEAVEN

The neighborhood soda fountain was a beloved haven of bygone days. Whether it was a gleaming marble creation—the pride of the local drugstore—or a festive counter in a main-street dime store, the town soda fountain had a unique atmosphere. It was a place where ordinary folk of all ages could relax and enjoy a special treat. Sodas and sundaes were concocted with the aid of brilliant dispensers, and flavored with colorful syrups before their very eyes. A simple and seductive pleasure indeed! Such sweet treats bring an innocent moment of magic into life—no wonder, then, that thoughts of soda fountains evoke longing, lingering, memories of a little piece of heaven.

> The crushed strawberries of ice cream soda places, the night wind in cottonwoods and willows, the lattice shadows of doorsteps and porches, these know more of the story.
>
> *Carl Sandburg*

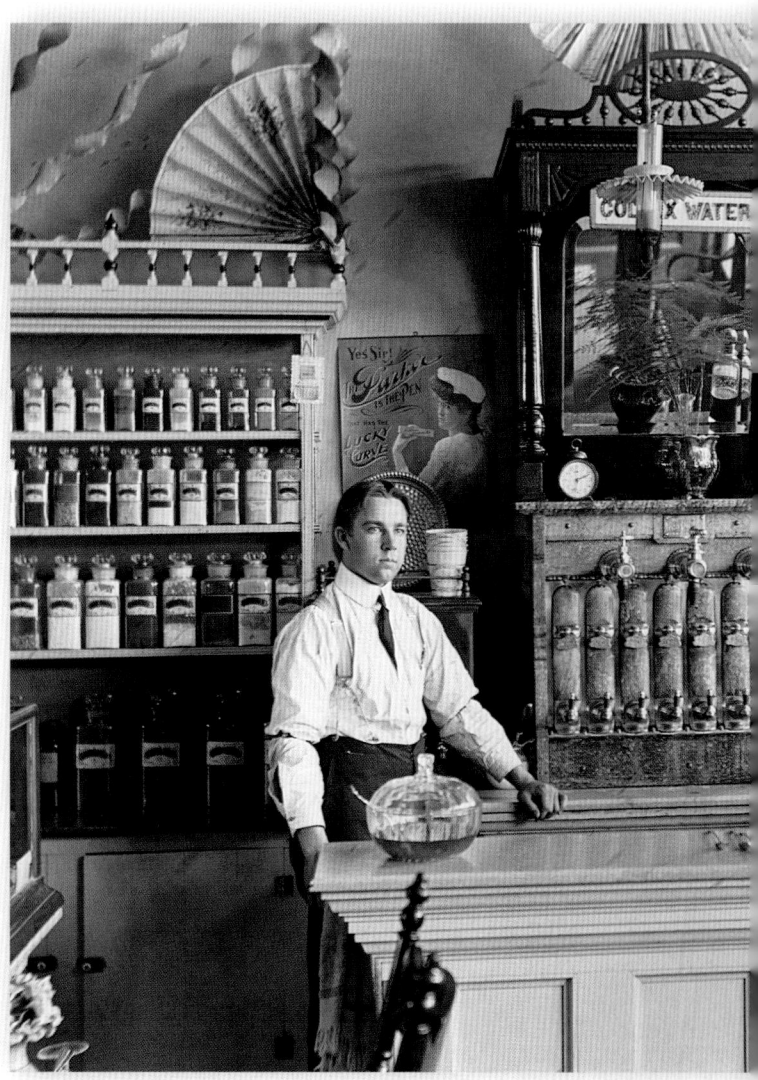

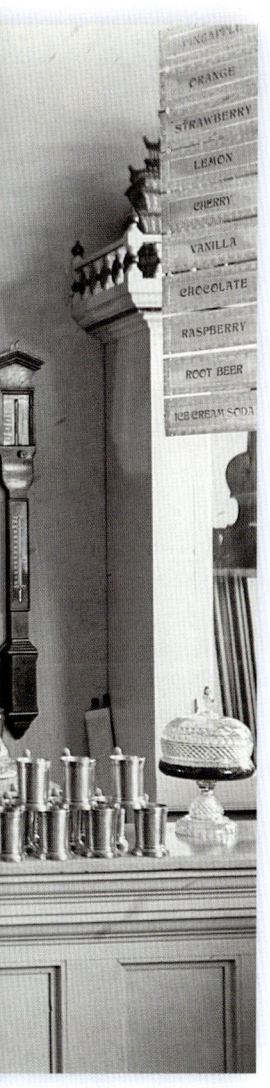

a little chaser

Soda water is closely connected to the healing powers of natural springs—in fact the earliest artificially made sodas were regarded as medicinal. That's why there has always been a close connection between drugstores and soda water. Various forms of soda fountains were patented and developed from the 1800s, and the familiar metal urns with their gooseneck spigots appeared in drugstores all over the United States. Pharmacists invented various flavorings, and offered special phosphate drinks as a chaser to take away the taste of the medicine the customer had just downed. These became so popular that customers came in and just asked for the "soda."

fairy-tale fountain

In a child's world, the most ordinary places become magical. For me, it was an ice cream parlor called The Buffalo Candy Kitchen, where I grew up in Kenosha, Wisconsin. It was on the east side of Main Street facing Market

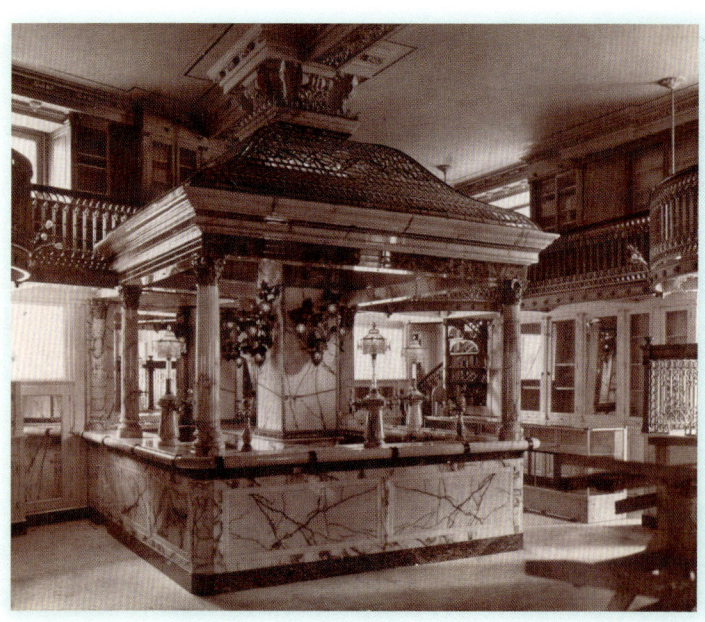

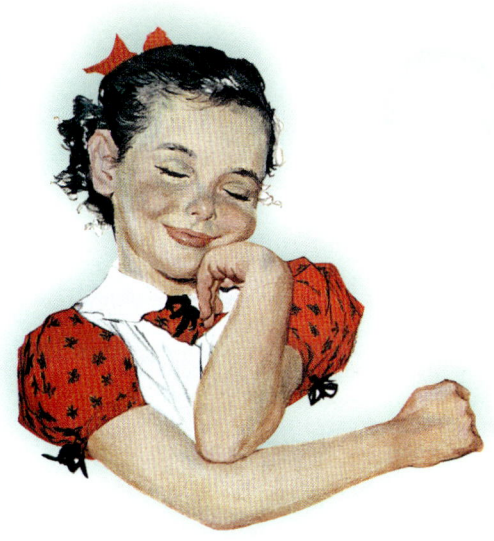

Square. The Buffalo was elegant. It was like a castle made of marble—marble on the counters and floors, marble-top tables and chairs. Against the walls were comfortable booths. The walls were paneled, and beautiful lanterns hung from them. The Art Deco-designed soda fountain had a root beer keg with a spigot. Faucets supplied the soda for fountain orders, and spigots the syrups for sundaes. During the summer, the white ceiling fans moved constantly. The delightful coolness and the natural chill of the marble attracted a lot of hot and thirsty customers.

Laverne Hammond

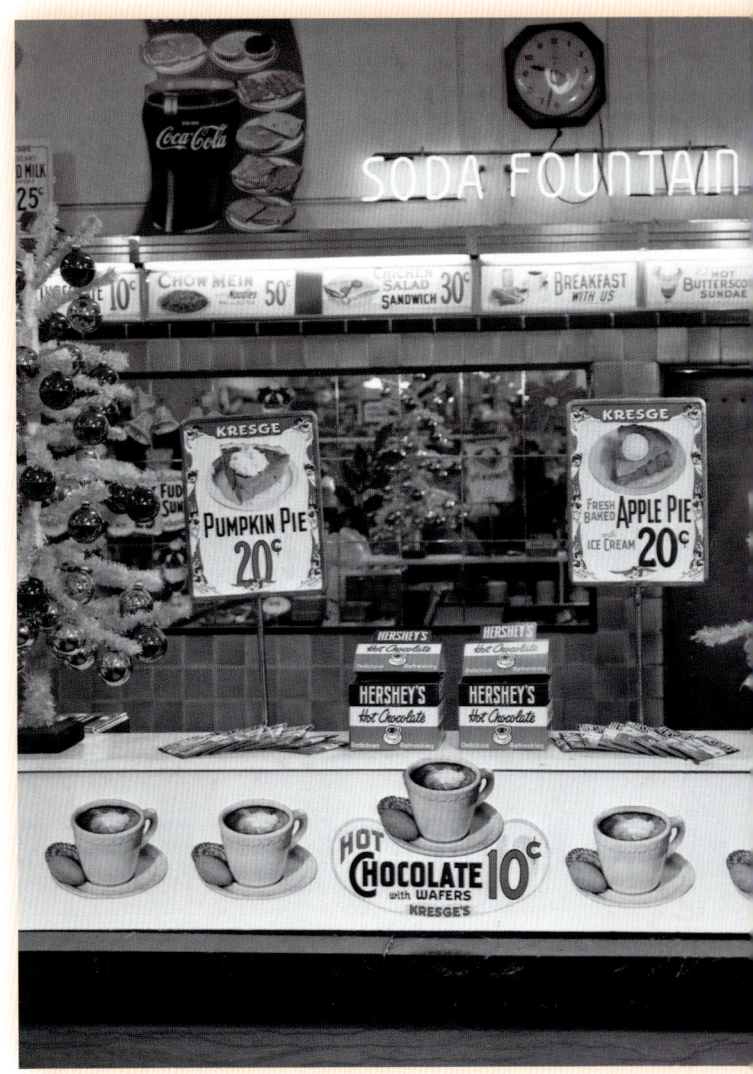

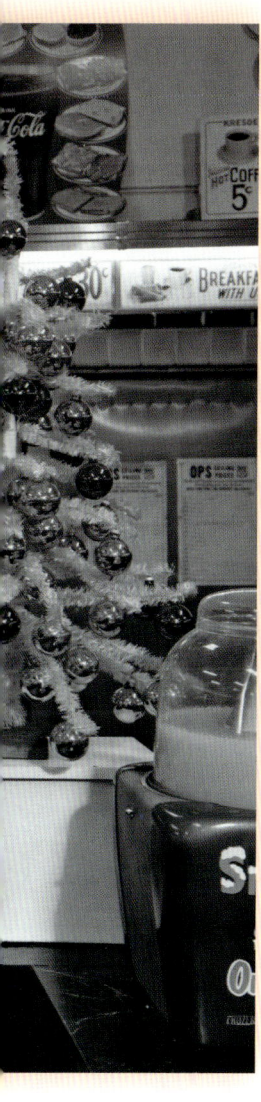

Christmas magic

I remember the beautiful Christmas decorations strung across Main Street. I remember the busy, busy sidewalks packed with folks shopping on a Friday evening. The sidewalk was so crowded that you could hardly make your way to the next store…There was a dime store in the 500 block on the square named Wiemans. There was a lunch counter at the rear of the store and you could get a lettuce and tomato sandwich for a quarter, and a small hot fudge for 35 cents. Soda was five cents a glass.

Marlene Huntley

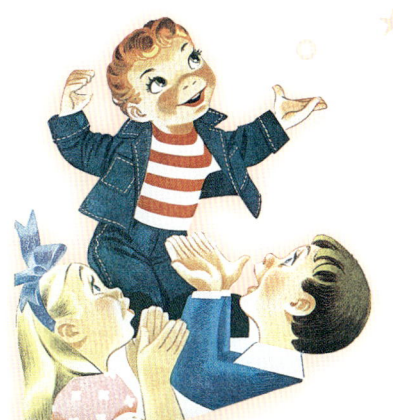

take your pick!

Us? Well, my family always went to the soda fountain at Ward's Drugs. My mom knew the soda jerk there way back from high school, I guess, and we stopped by most Saturdays to see what they had in. While they were talking, I'd check out the candy! Nesco's were my favorite, I recall. Anyway, she'd let me take my pick from the soda fountain—but I knew not to spend a lot—we didn't have much money then. Well, the nice thing was, they always added a bit extra—some nuts, or an extra squirt of flavoring if you wanted it.

Will Evans

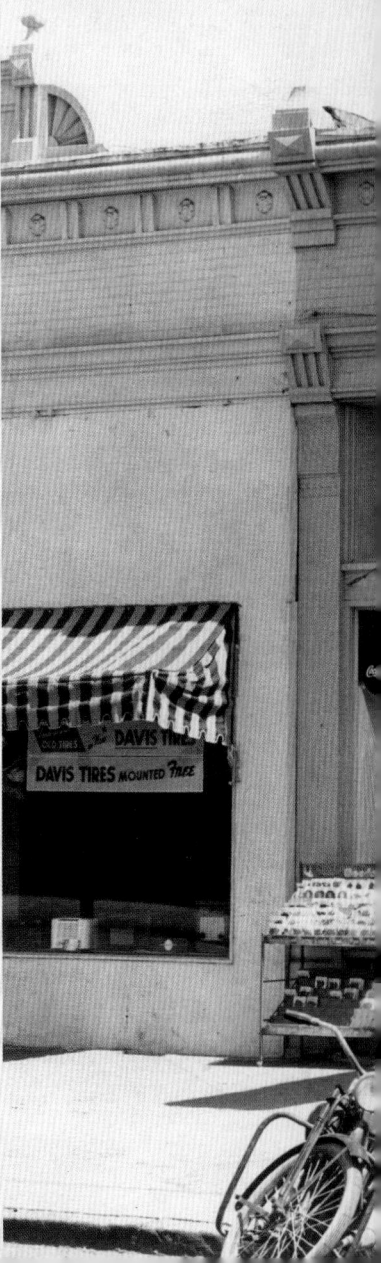

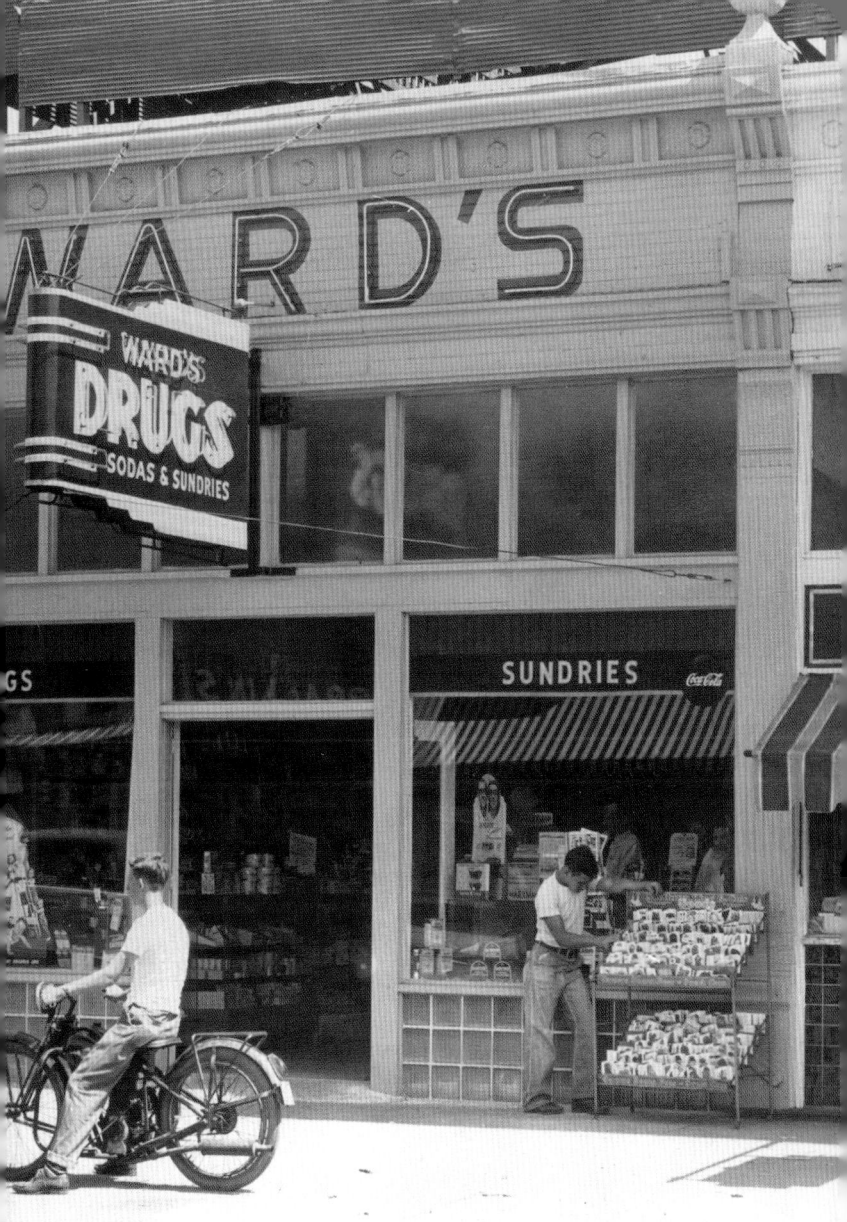

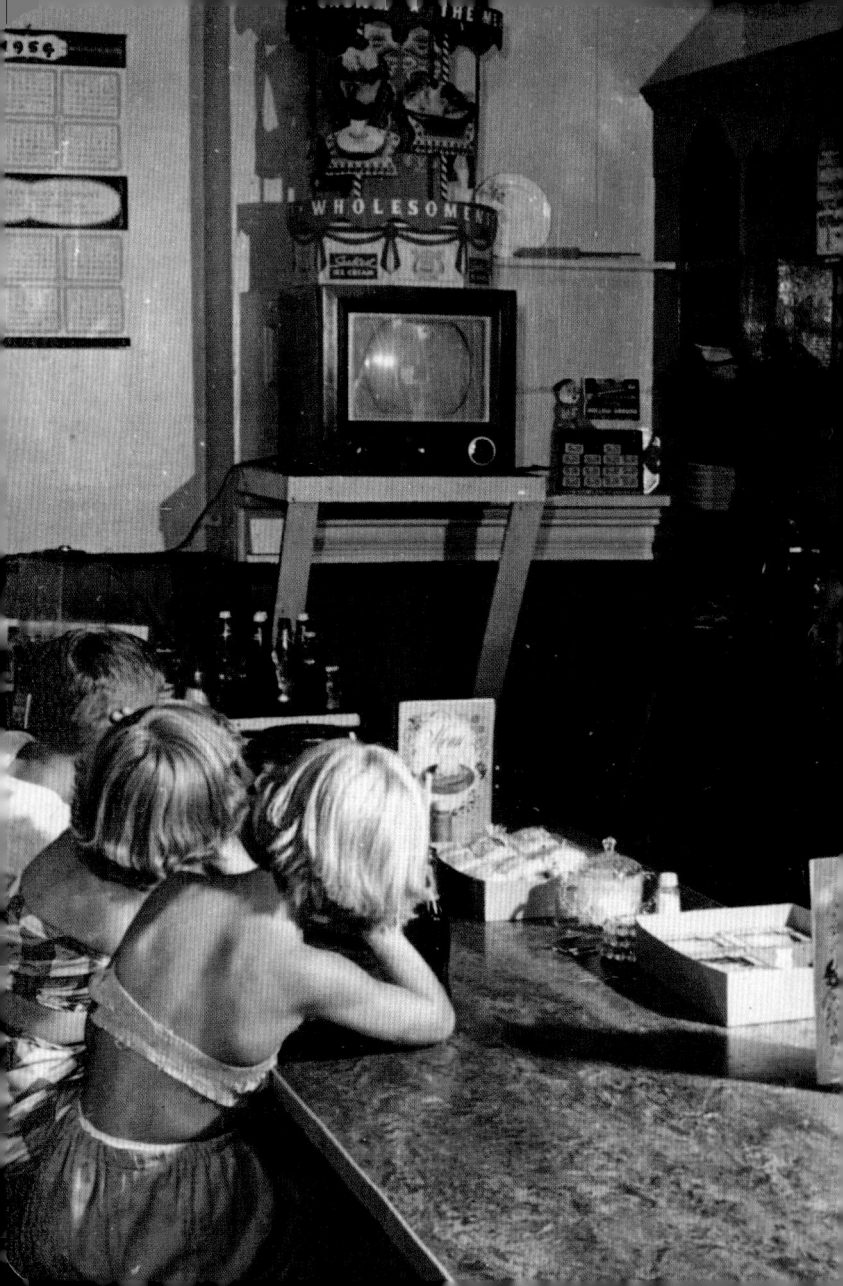

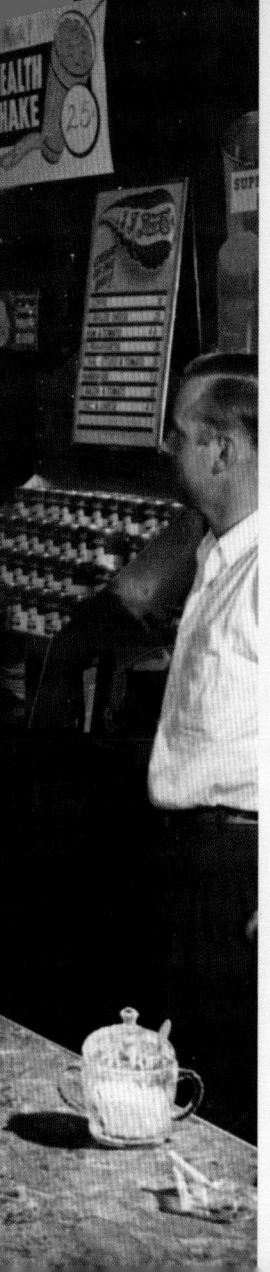

a little extra

One of the strongest memories I have from being a kid in Kansas City, Missouri in the 1950s is how long the summers were then, and how nice and cool it was at our drugstore soda fountain. You could whirl around on the stools, but the owner would give you a funny look if you did that too much. So you did it when he wasn't looking. We all used to go there after school and he'd fix us cherry Cokes, vanilla Cokes, ice cream sodas, chocolate malts, whatever we wanted. The drinks didn't cost all that much, and I especially liked the phosphates. They had a high school student working there sometimes, and when he was in a good mood he would put in some extra flavoring and say it was for good behavior!

Lynne Dowling

drinks for a penny

Our "spa" in the 1950s was, in those days, a candy store with a soda fountain. There we delighted in a 2-cent plain (a large glass of seltzer) or fruit drinks for a penny made of syrup in containers with a spigot holding green (lemon/lime), red (cherry), and orange.

Phyllis Prussick

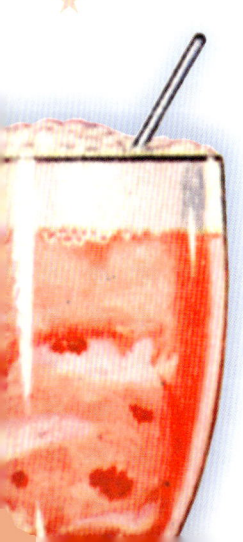

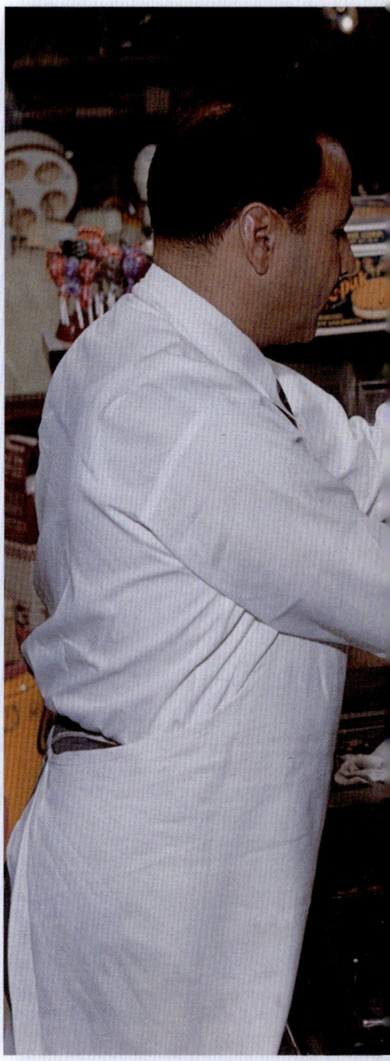

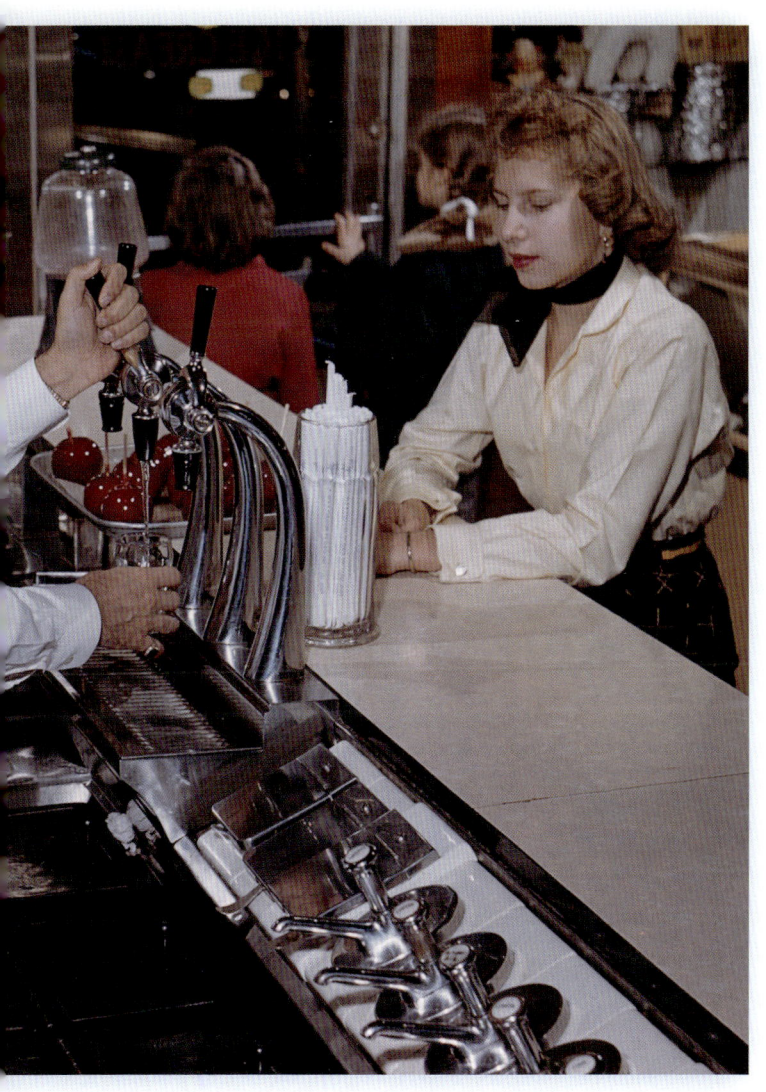

my blue heaven

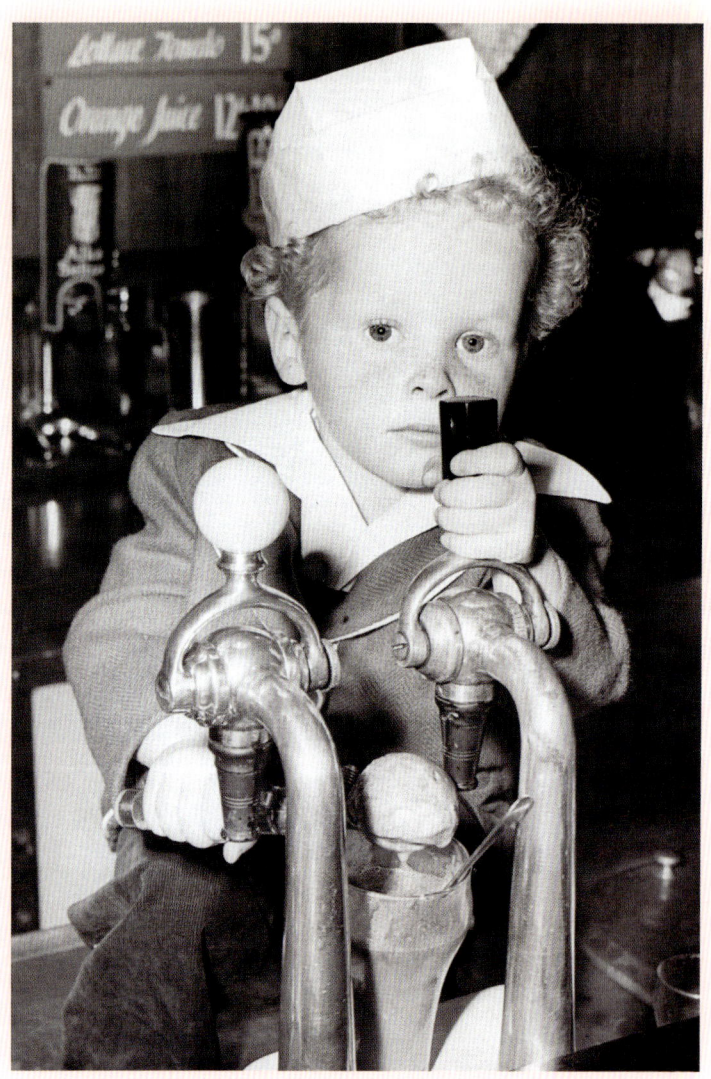

My mental images of Wichita Falls in the early '50s are as monochromatic as the Brownie Box snapshot of a 4-year-old self, clutching my grandmother's hand and looking bewilderingly lost in a forest of overcoat tails…

I endured the seemingly endless waiting in countless dress shops and shoe stores that lined Scott and Indiana Streets back then, knowing that eventually we would make our way to the really important parts of the trip, the dime stores…

that first strawberry malt

Another highlight was City Drug with its impressive soda fountain, echoing hardwood floor, slow-turning ceiling fans, and exotic aromas. Here I tasted my first strawberry malt and became addicted for life.

Jim Miller

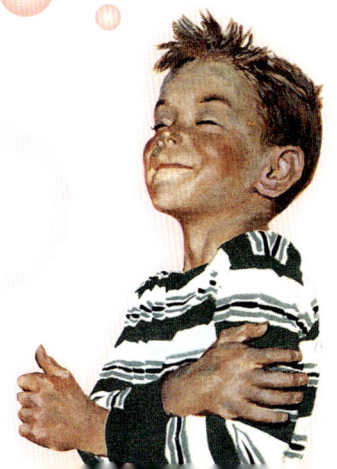

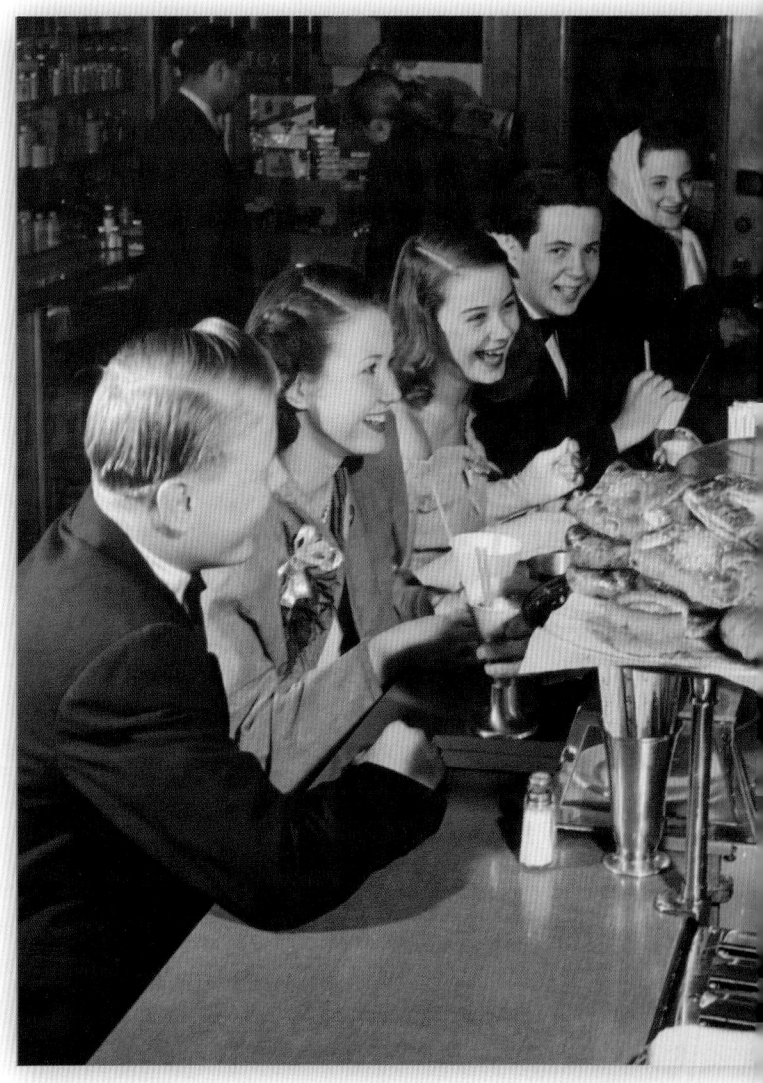

such a happy place

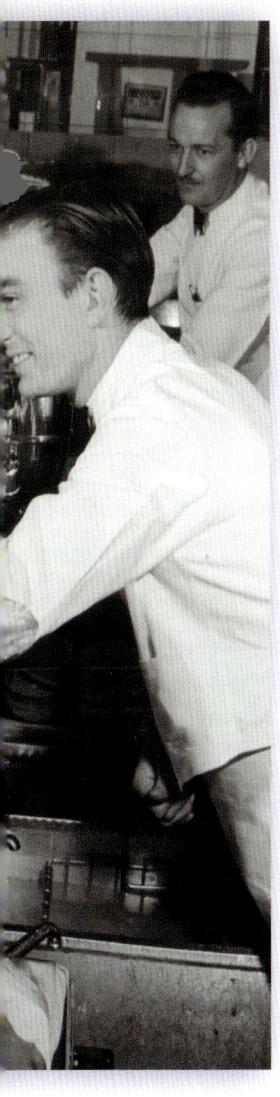

On a warm August evening the drug store of Mariposa, as you know, is all a blaze of lights. You can hear the hissing of the soda-water fountain half a block away, and inside the store there are ever so many people—boys and girls and old people too—all drinking sarsaparilla and chocolate sundaes and lemon sours and foaming drinks that you take out of long straws. There is such a laughing and a talking as you never heard, and the girls are all in white and pink and Cambridge blue, and the soda fountain is of white marble with silver taps, and it hisses and sputters, and Jim Eliot and his assistant wear white coats with red geraniums in them, and it's just as gay as gay.

Stephen Leacock

The main problem I had was that there was so much choice. Our soda fountain displayed bright color pictures of all the main attractions, like pineapple sundaes, banana splits, chocolate malts, tutti-fruttis, that kind of thing. Then there was the menu to consider—there was a lot more on offer there. Also, how much money did I have in my pocket? Could I afford a sundae and a soda as well? Maybe, if I had the small size of each? Or just a dish of ice cream, and a soda or phosphate? But what flavor? Lemon, cherry, lime, vanilla, grape? You could say we were spoilt for choice, and you'd be quite right!

Jeannie Wilson

menu delights

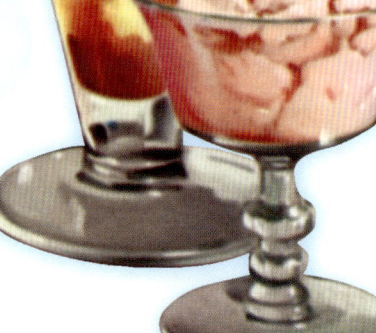

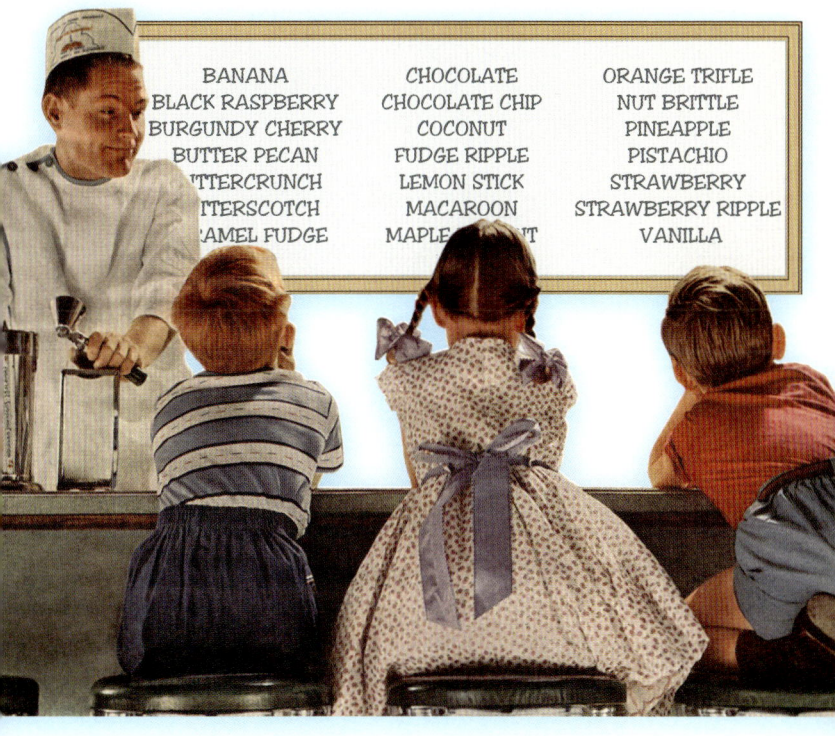

Chapter 2
TUTTI-FRUTTI

Few memories are as pleasurably evocative as the recollection of your first banana split, pineapple sundae, or tutti-frutti. Pure delight! And the fairy-tale atmosphere of the soda fountain, with its cool, marble top, and gleaming chrome fittings made the anticipation of these delicious confections even more exciting. First the ice cream—sumptuous helpings piled into a shiny glass or silver dish, and smothered in generous servings of fruit, chocolate, or fudge syrup. Then a dollop of luxurious whipped cream, and a final sprinkling of chopped nuts. Sheer, unabashed indulgence, eaten with a special little silver ice cream spoon to make the treat complete.

We dare not trust our wit for making our house pleasant to our friends, so we buy ice cream.

Ralph Waldo Emerson

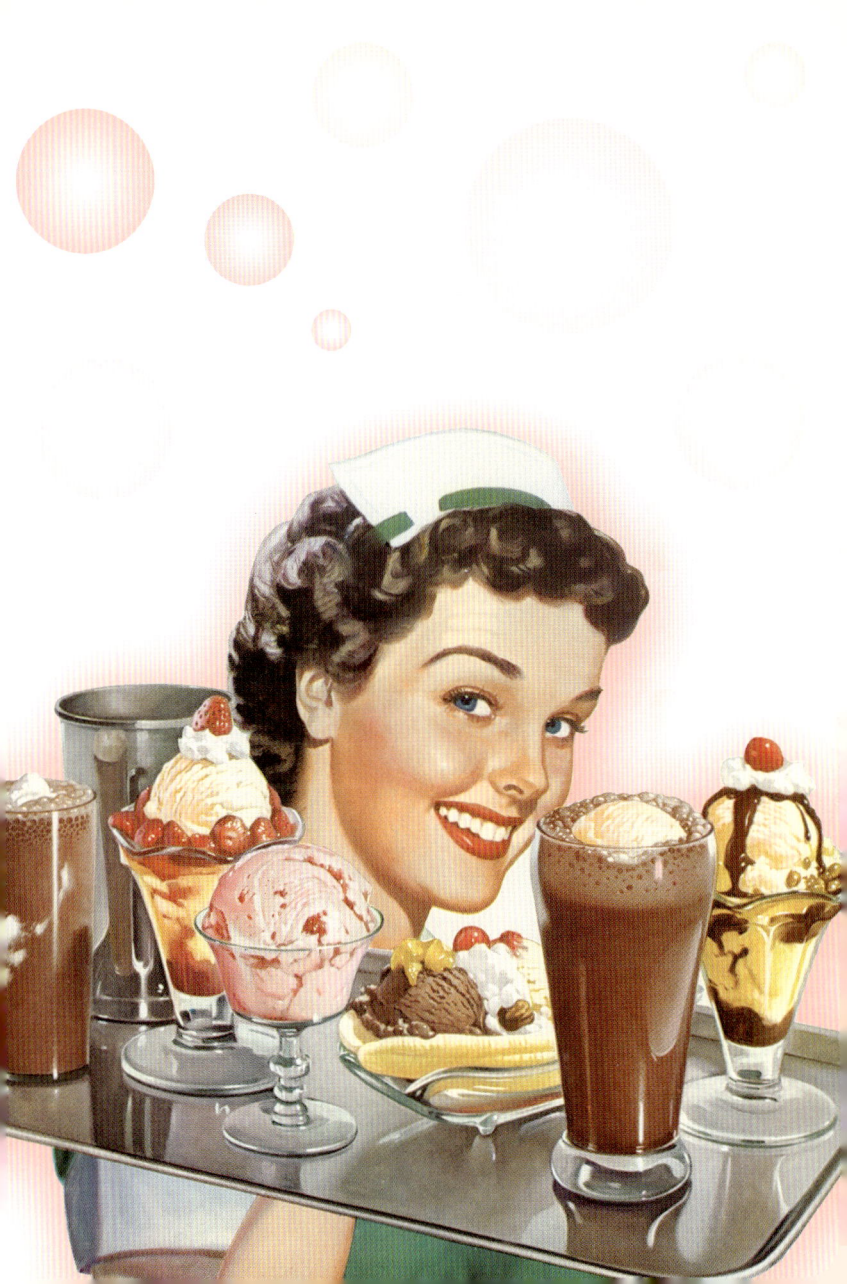

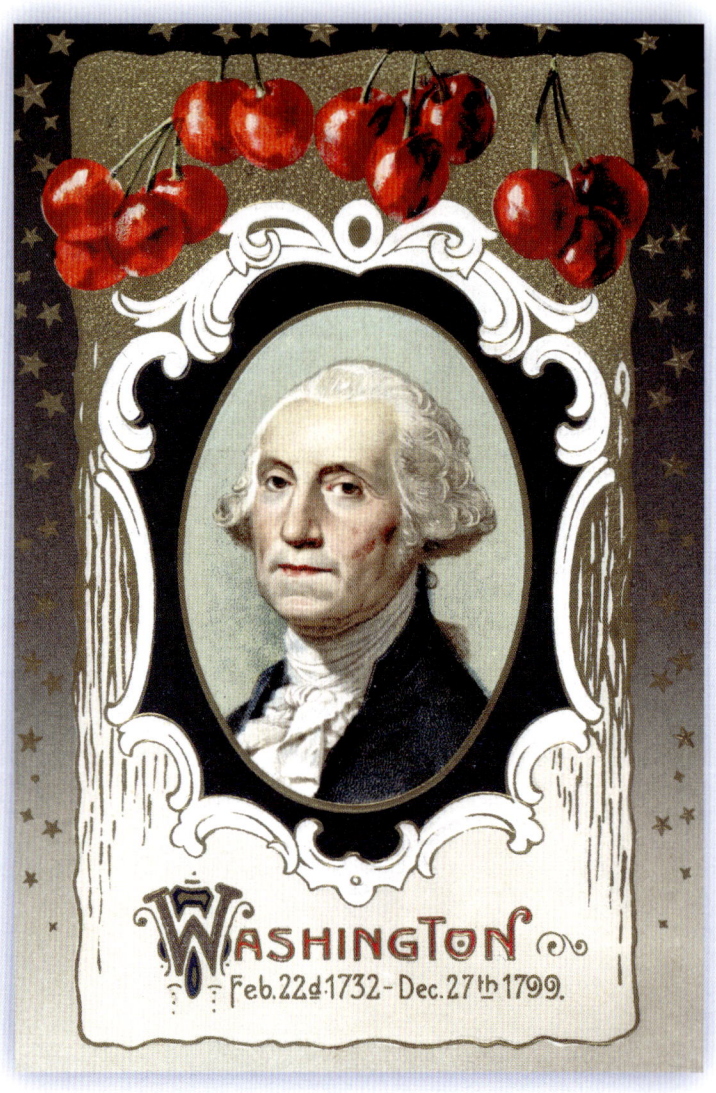

ice cream moments

- The first recorded reference to ice cream in the United States was found in a journal of Maryland's governor, Thomas Bladen. The entry, dated 1744, described a dinner party at his home. The dessert was ice cream made with milk and strawberries.

- Ice cream was a favorite dessert of American presidents George Washington, Thomas Jefferson, and James Madison. During the summer of 1790, Washington ordered $200 worth of the cooling treat—this would be the equivalent of about $96,400 today!

- The patent for the first hand-cranked ice cream freezer was awarded to Nancy M. Johnson in 1843. She sold it later for just $1500.

- Jacob Fussell founded the first commercial ice cream plant in America in 1851—he has sometimes been called the "father" of the ice cream industry.

- A law introduced in Newark, New Jersey, in the nineteenth century, banned the sale of ice cream after 6 p.m. if the customer did not have a doctor's signed note of consent.

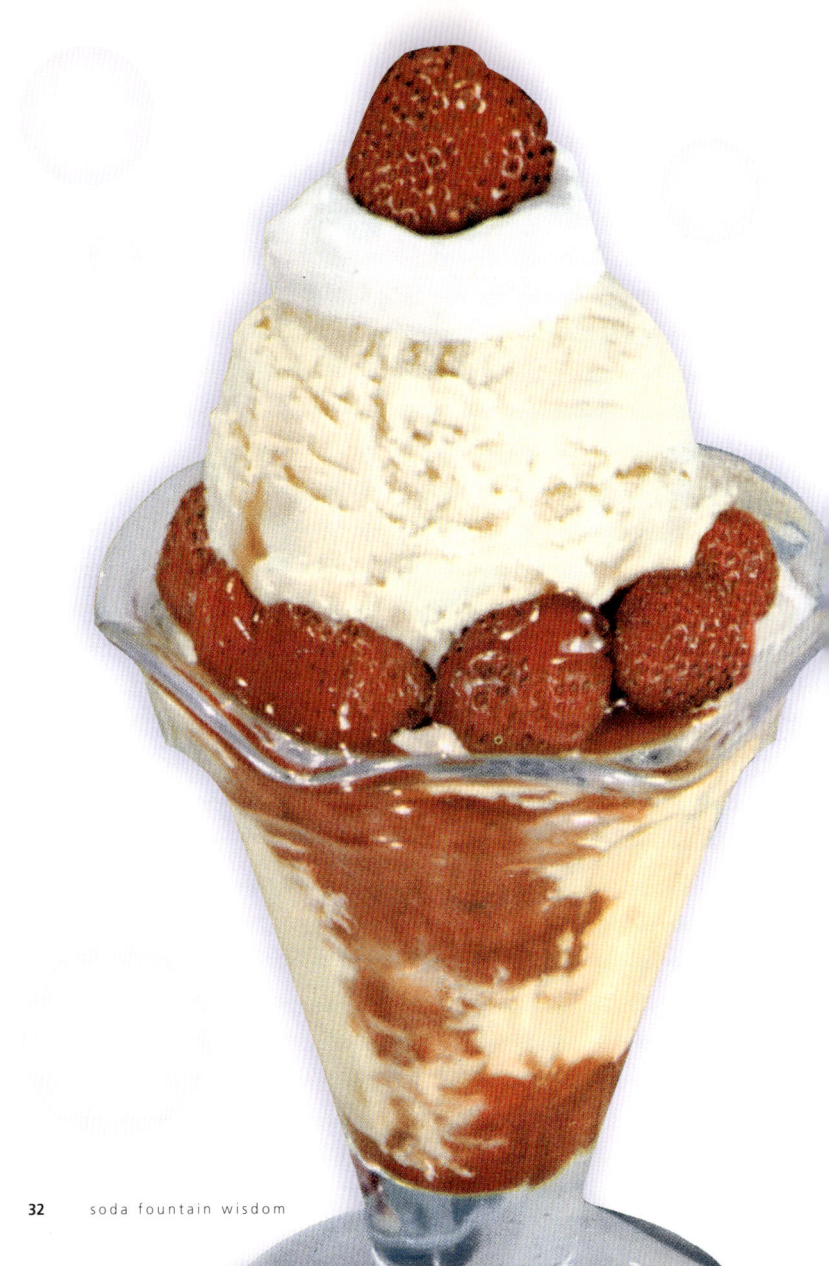

never on a Sunday

In the late nineteenth century Evanston, Illinois, nicknamed "Heavenston" by Frances Willard, was a Methodist-minded town, so pious that the town fathers, resenting the dissipating influence of the soda fountain, passed an ordinance forbidding the sale of ice cream sodas on Sunday. Some ingenious confectioners, obeying the law, served ice cream with syrup but no soda. This sodaless soda was the Sunday soda, and became so popular that orders for "Sundays" crossed the counter every day of the week. When objection was raised to christening the dish after the Sabbath, the spelling was changed to Sundae, and so developed one of America's most characteristic dishes.

William Lyon Phelps

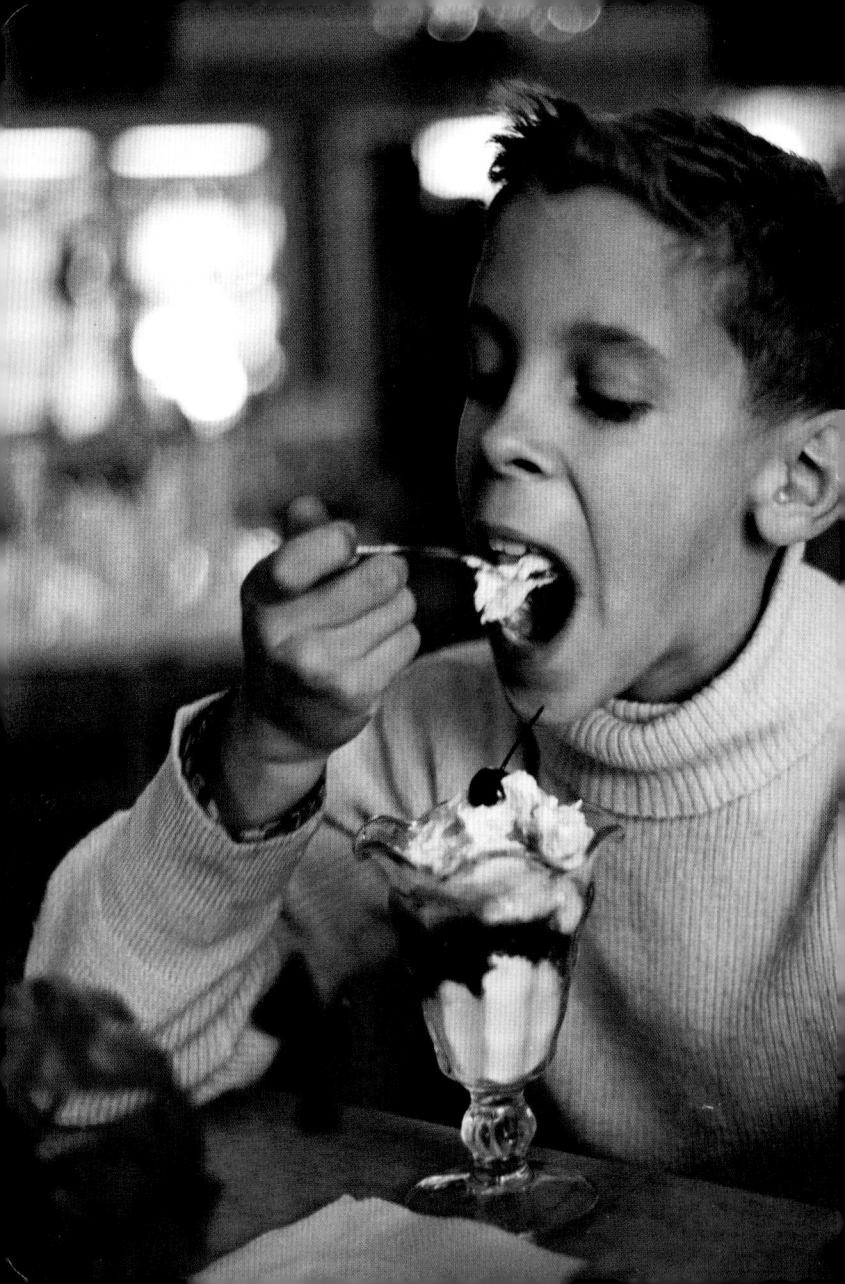

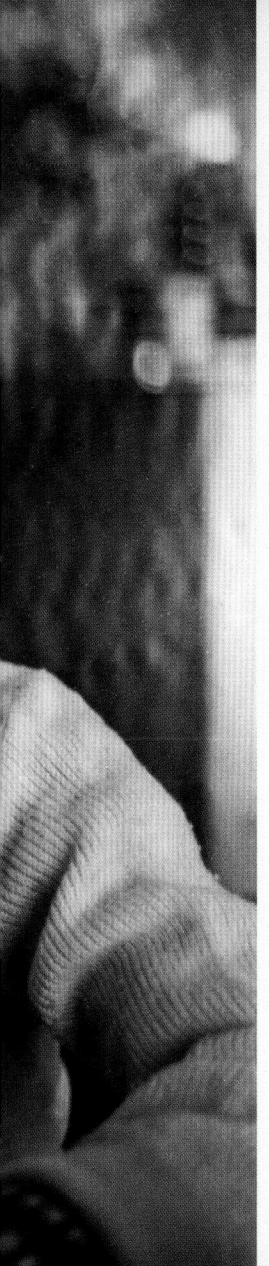

first sundae—the official version?

About 45 years ago, on a Sunday afternoon, John M. Scott, then pastor of the Unitarian Church, and Chester Platt were having their usual Sunday confab in back of the prescription counter, when Mr. Platt proposed that they have some refreshment. Mr. Platt then came up to the counter where I was holding forth, asking for two dishes of ice cream, and on each he placed a candied cherry. Then, after considering a bit, he poured cherry syrup all over them, making a very attractive-looking dessert. When he and Mr. Scott tried out this new concoction, they became very enthusiastic about its flavor and appearance, and immediately started casting about for a suitable name for it. It was then that Mr. Scott said, why not call it Cherry Sunday in commemoration of the day on which it was invented?

DeForest Christiance

A visit to the Buffalo Candy Kitchen was a treat for my brother and me…I will never forget the Battleship Sundae, one of the fancier dishes. It was the second most expensive item on the menu. It cost 50 cents! Three scoops of flavored ice creams were served in a chrome boat. Three sauces covered each scoop, topped with a dollop of real whipped cream. Finally, the entire treat was topped by a generous sprinkling of chopped nuts. This special sundae came adorned with an American flag. The most expensive item on the menu was the banana split. It was similar to the Battleship, except that it had a banana sliced lengthwise in the boat and no flag. Adding a banana cost 75 cents.

Laverne Hammond

Battleship Special

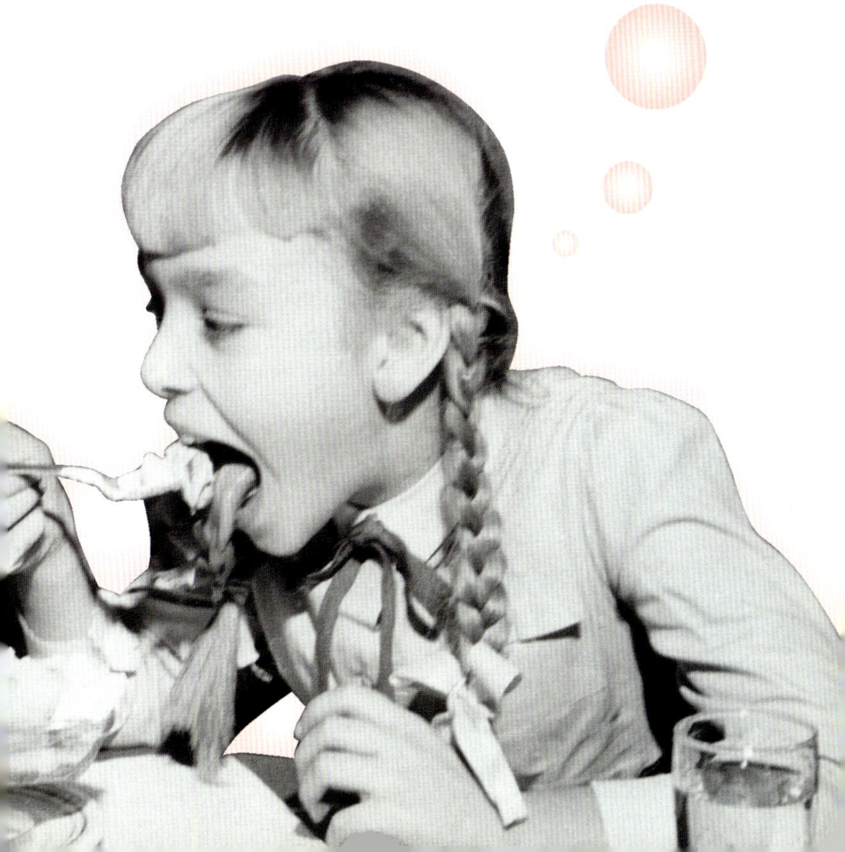

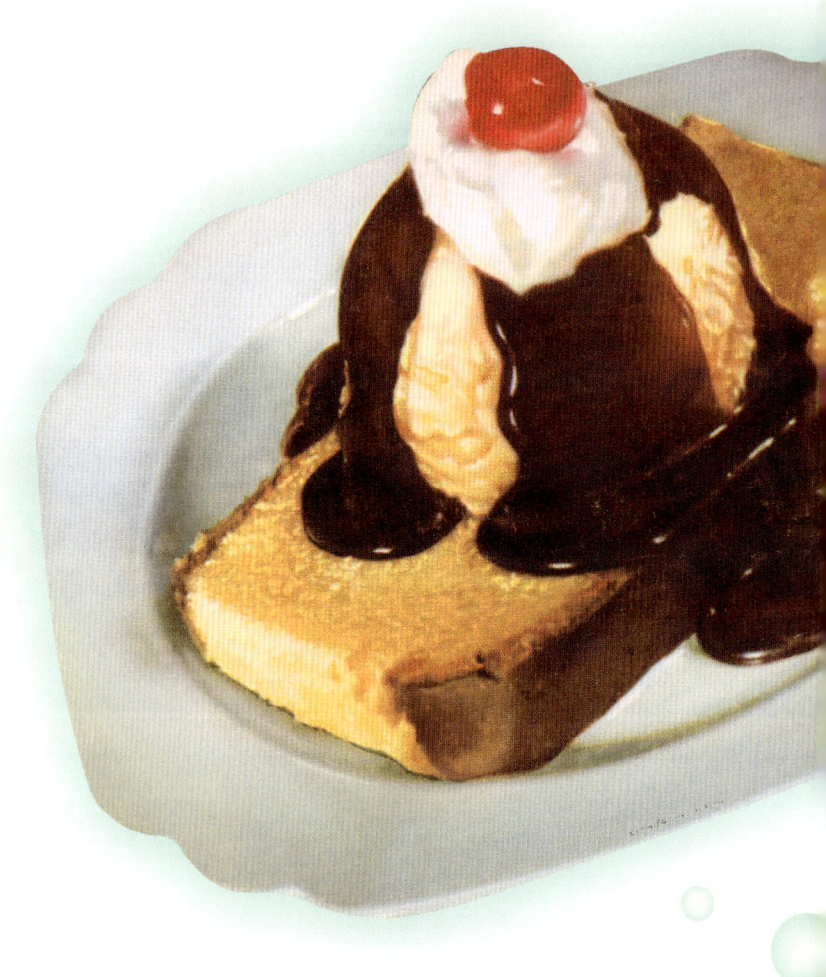

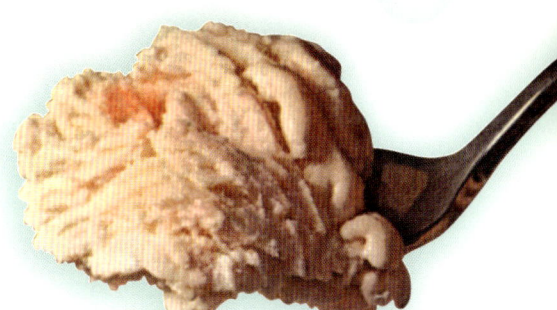

"Ice cream
is generally eaten
with a spoon, but when
accompanied by cake,
either the spoon alone
or both the spoon and
fork may be used."

Emily Post

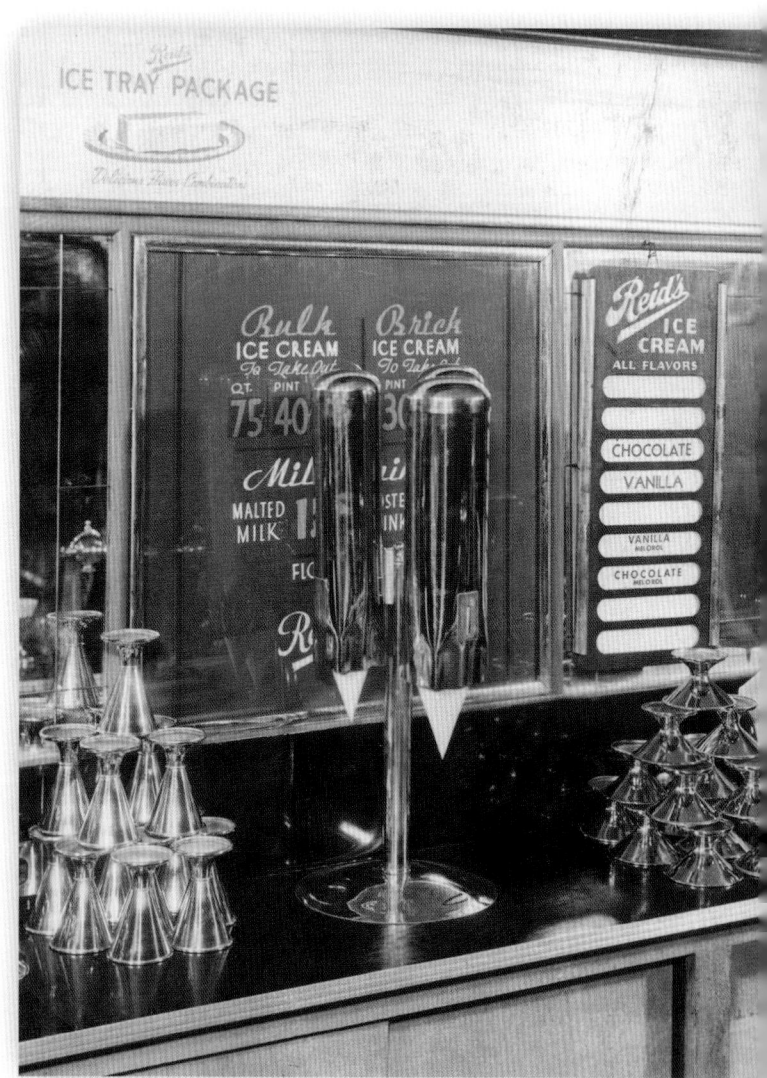

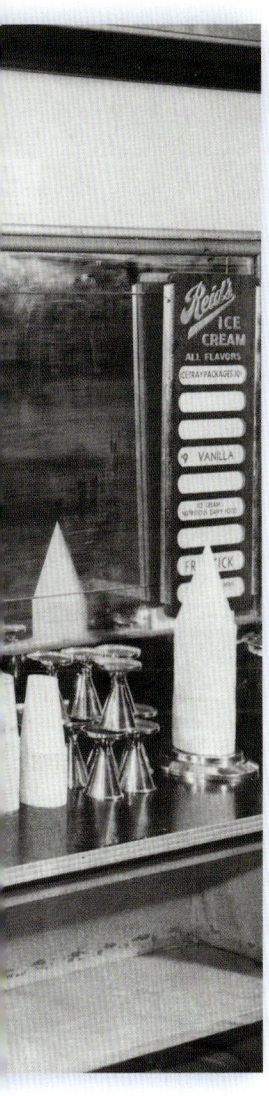

just marvelous!

…we went to the People's Drugstore, which was at the corner of Portland Street across the street from the Congress Theater. They had a soda fountain and our favorite sundae was chocolate ice cream with marshmallow sauce. It was served in a beautiful pressed steel sundae glass which would be so cold because they kept it in the freezer box. It was just marvelous. It cost fifteen cents, which was a little much for us, so we didn't get that very often. We tried to get a lot of money together so each of us could get our own. We collected bottles to trade in for money. The soda bottles were two cents and the quart bottles were a nickel.

Tom Reese

My first stop after the day's classes were over was the Jayhawk soda fountain. I'd sit for a while at the counter, chatting to the soda jerk, and looking at the neat pictures they had tacked up on the wall showing all the fountain specials.

"I just love that cherry pie!"

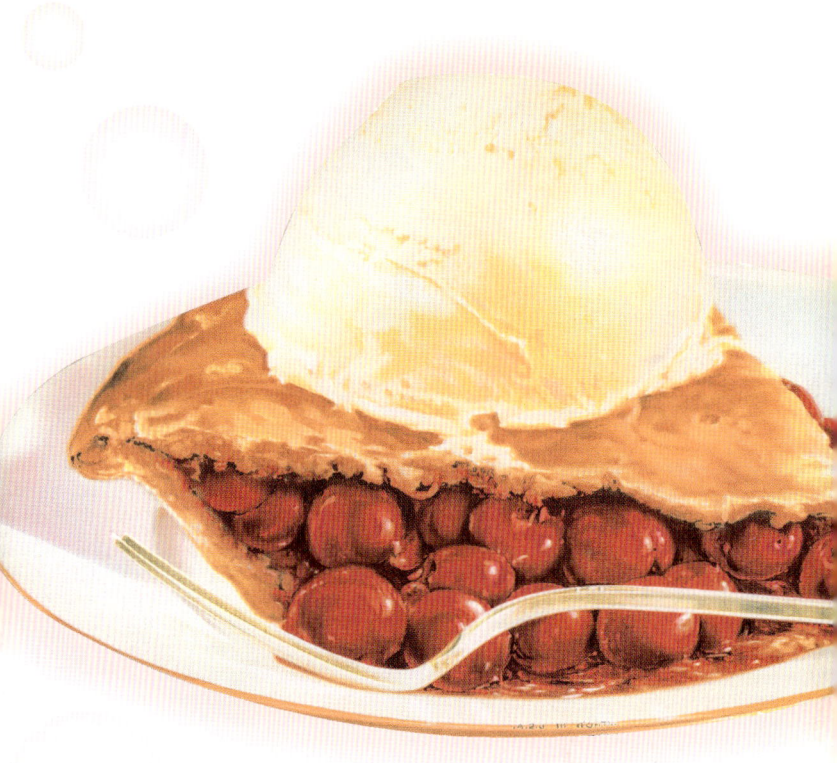

I have to say that my favorite treat was a slice of cherry pie and a scoop of vanilla ice cream. I just loved that combination of flavors. I guess I must have tried every dish they had, but I never did like anything better than that pie. And soda? Well, if I had a few extra cents, I'd get a cherry Coke to go with it. That was just heaven, I thought.

Bebe James

"My advice to you is not to inquire why or whither, but just enjoy your ice cream while it's on your plate—that's my philosophy."

Thornton Wilder

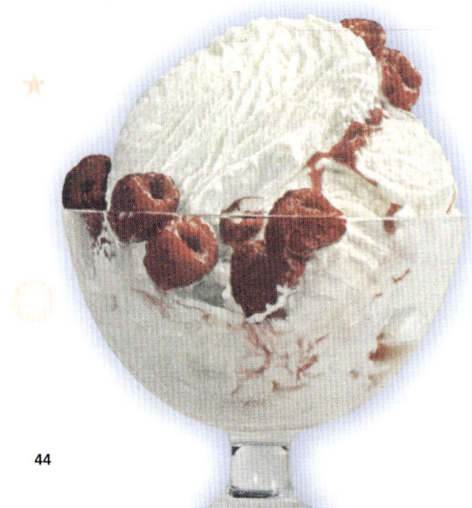
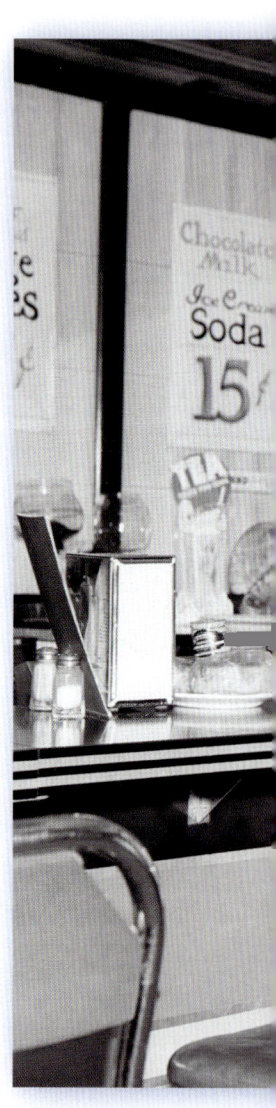

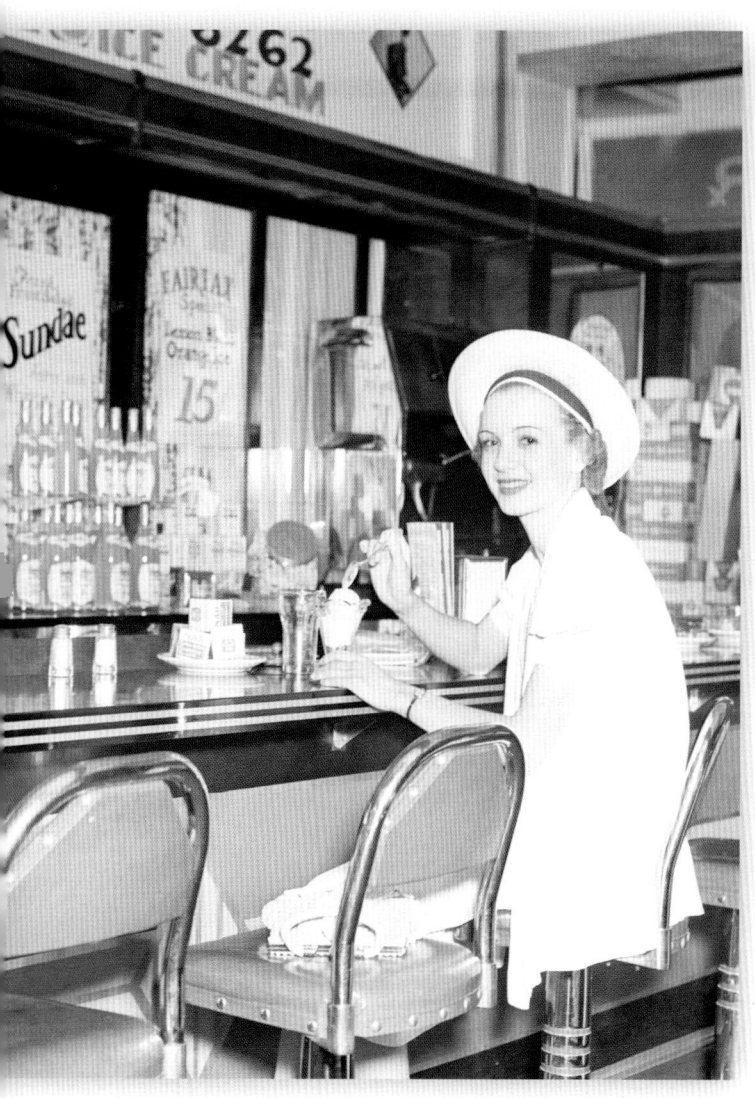

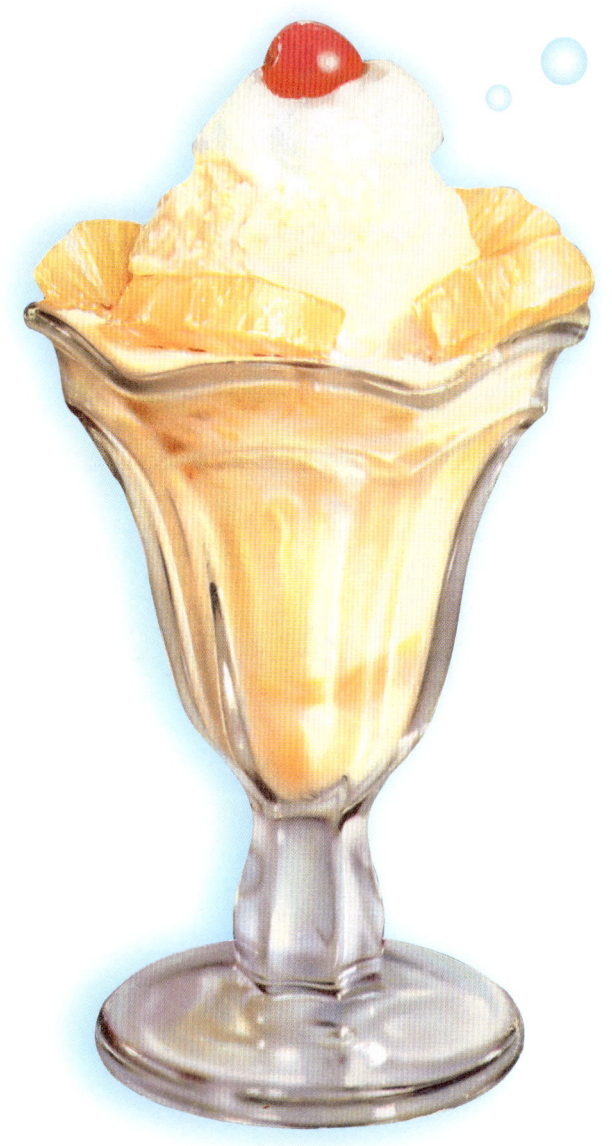

Pineapple Sundae

¹/₄ cup (60 ml.) pineapple syrup
2 scoops vanilla ice cream
6 segments fresh pineapple
dollop whipped cream
maraschino cherry, to decorate

1 Pour half of the pineapple syrup into the bottom of a traditional sundae glass.

2 Add the ice cream and top with the remaining syrup

3 Place the pineapple segments around the rim of the glass. Add the whipped cream, and decorate with the maraschino cherry.

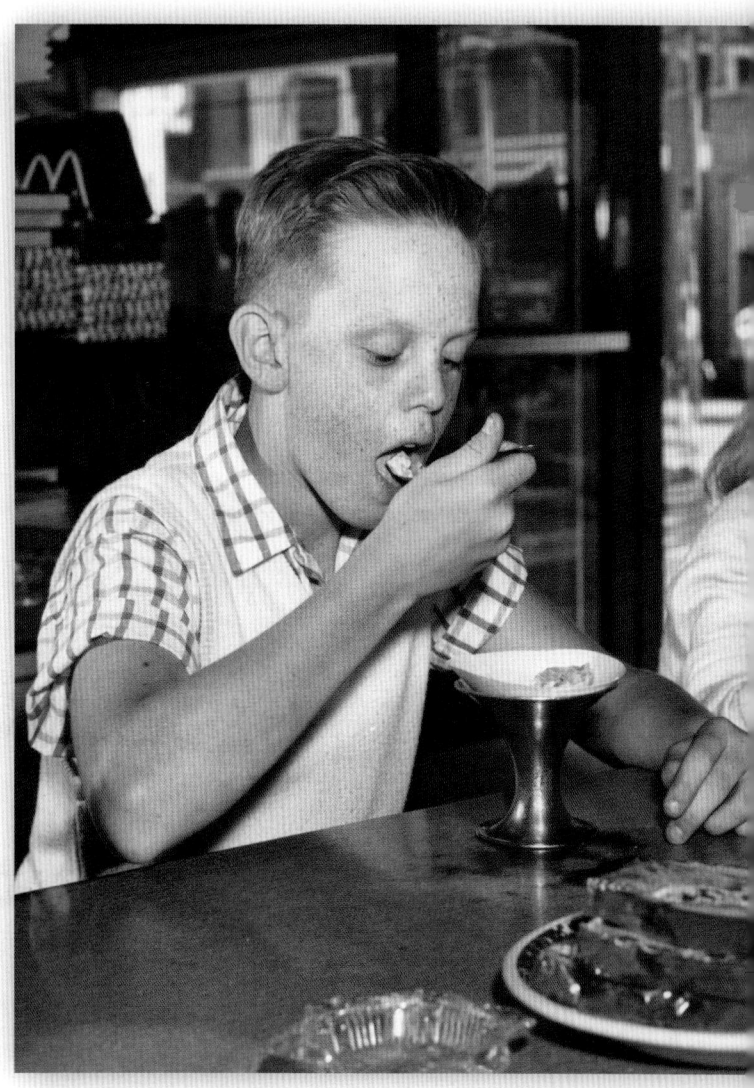

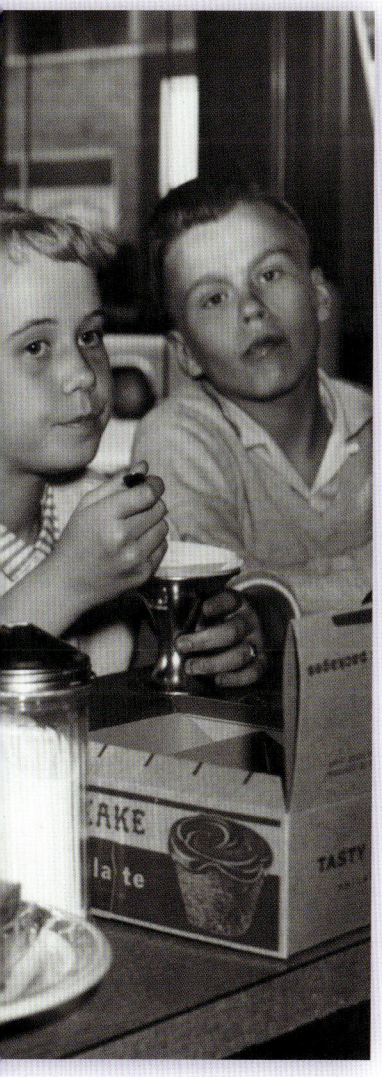

homemade sweet treats

Our favorite soda fountain where we lived in St. Louis was Walgreens, and we used to hang out there for hours on end. We'd check out the latest comics, and make our sodas and phosphates last as long as possible. They had every kind of ice cream you could think of, as well as fresh, homemade fruitcake, cookies and brownies. All served with vanilla ice cream, whipped cream, whatever you wanted. Well, they were the best, and we didn't even think of going anywhere else.

Charlie Dunwell

"Always serve too much hot fudge sauce on hot fudge sundaes. It makes people overjoyed, and puts them in your debt."

Judith Olney

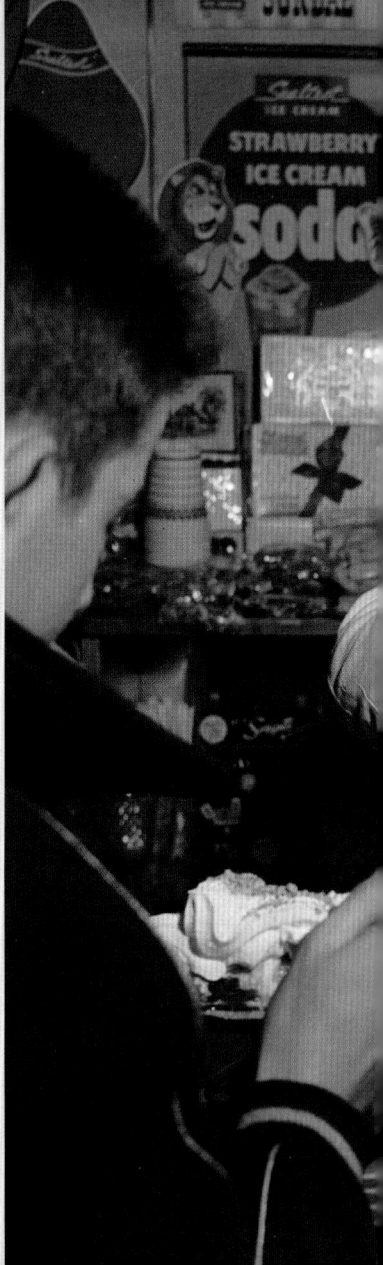

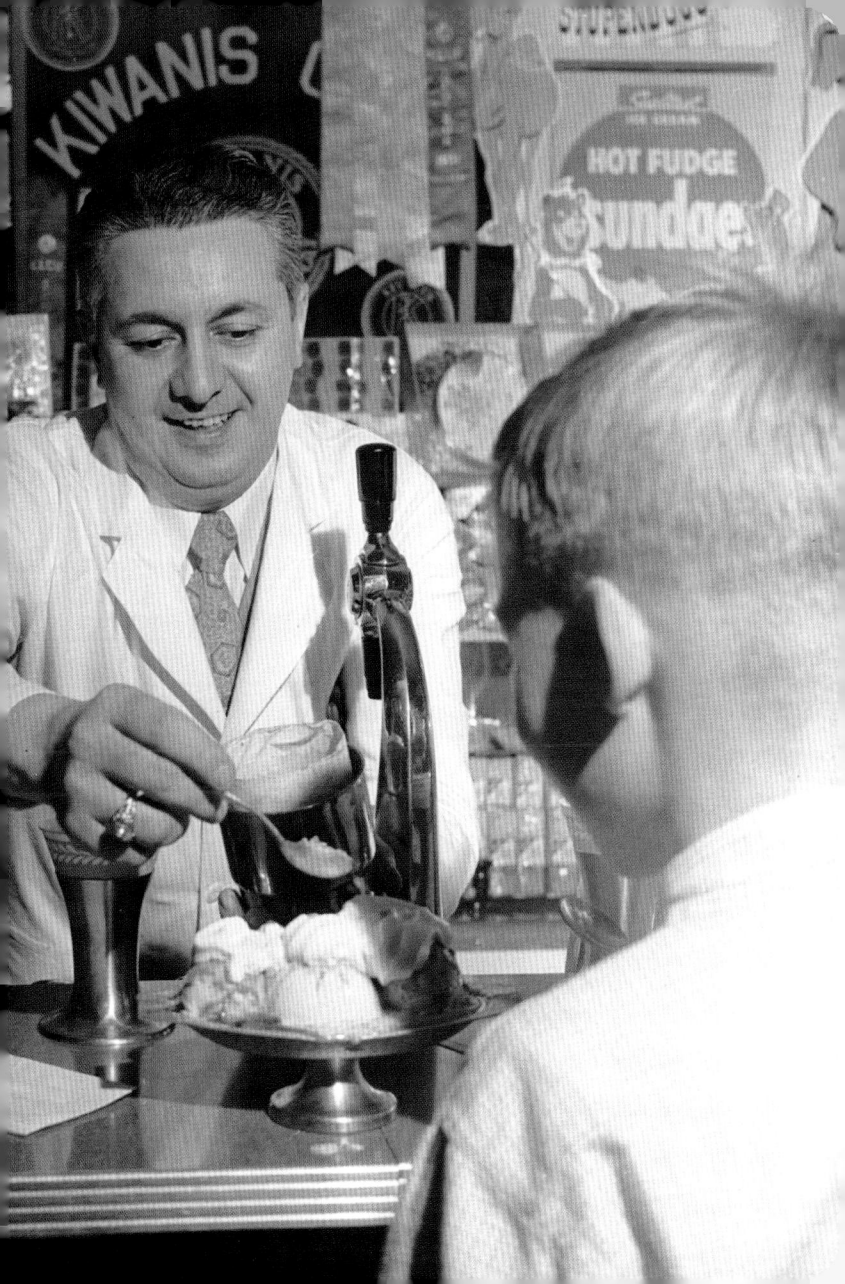

hurrah for ice cream!

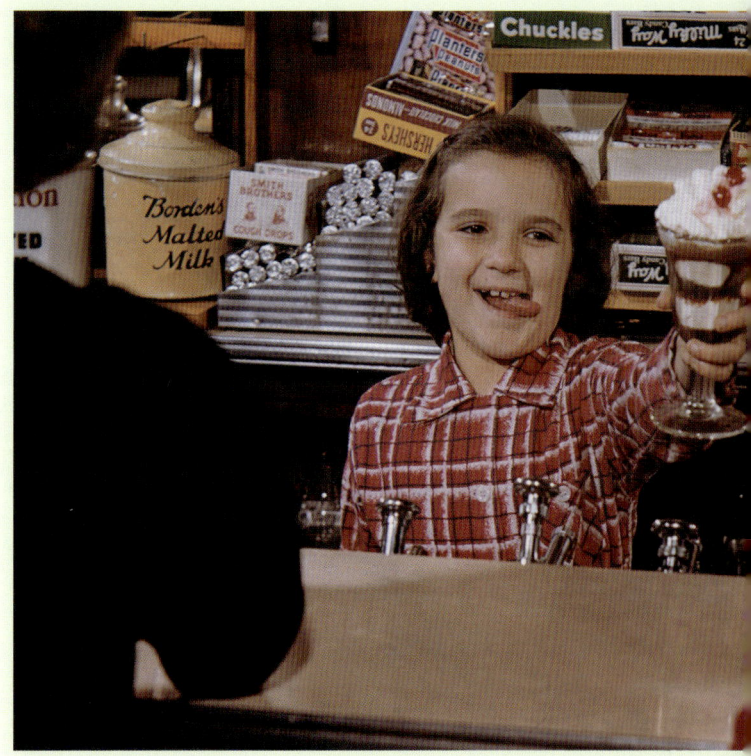

52 soda fountain wisdom

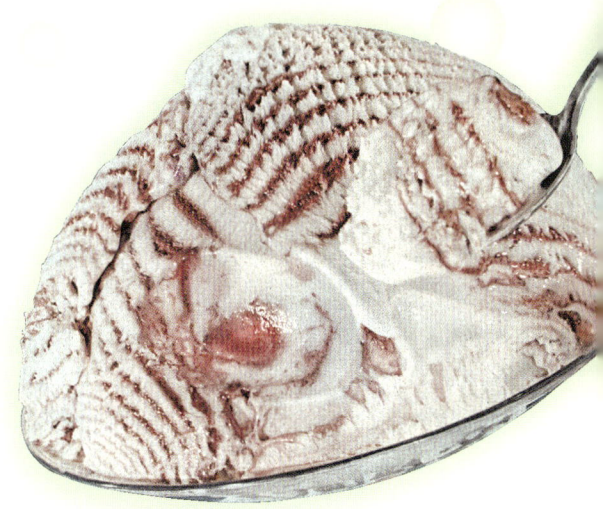
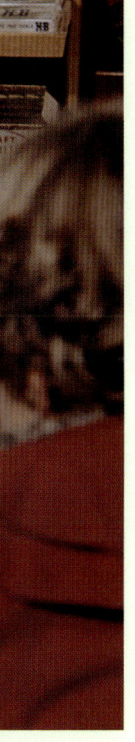

"You scream, I scream,
they all scream
for ice cream.
Tuesdays, Mondays,
They all scream
for sundaes."

University of Kansas cheer (1920s)

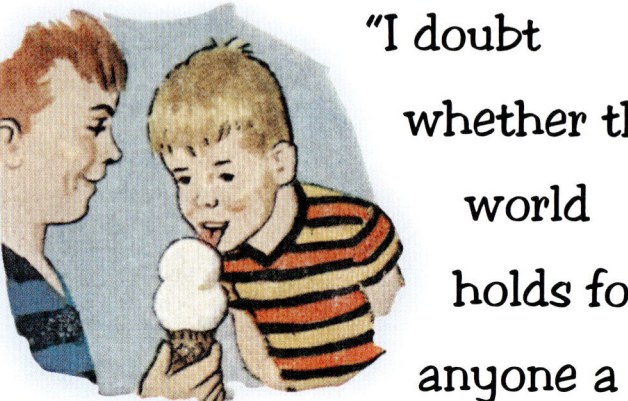

"I doubt whether the world holds for anyone a more soul-stirring surprise than the first adventure with ice cream."

Heywood Campbell Brown

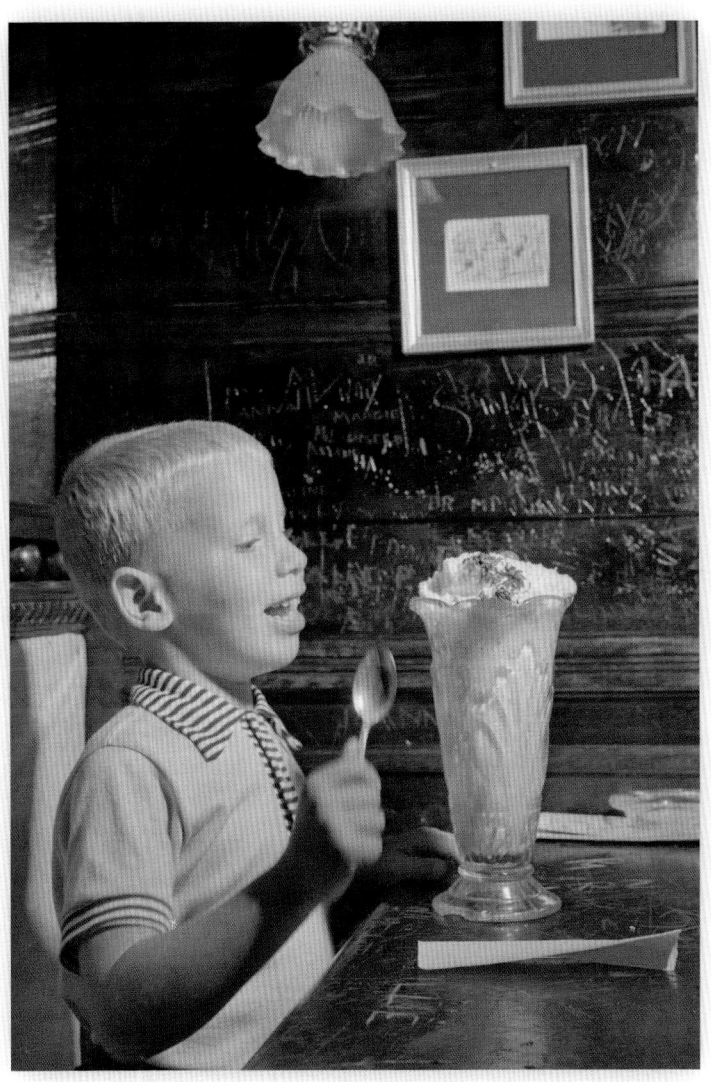

I was the one kid in my family who was a really fanatical ice cream hound—I just couldn't get enough. I told the soda jerk at Ward's drugstore that I was going to take over his job as soon as I was old enough. He just laughed. I always remember the TV commercial with these cute puppets called Kukla and Ollie singing the praises of Sealtest ice cream. I used to join right in on the beat when they chorused "Delicious! Mmmm! And so delightful!" Then I used to give my mom this pleading look and she'd shake her head meaning "later." Kukla and Ollie were really funny—they even had their own TV show. We all watched them, they were very popular at the time

Danny Edwards

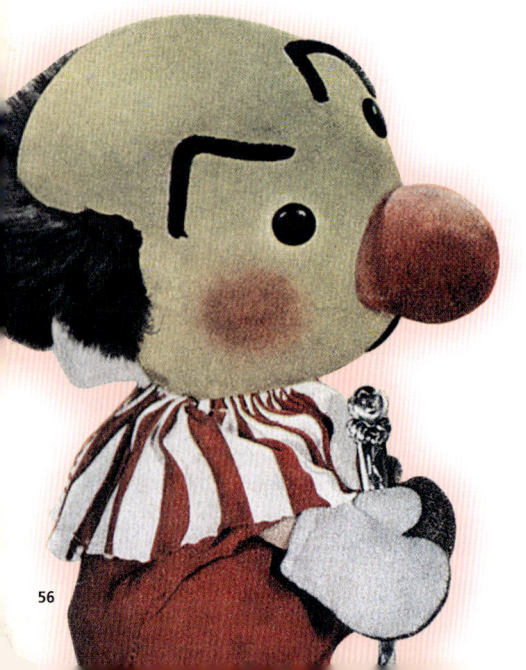

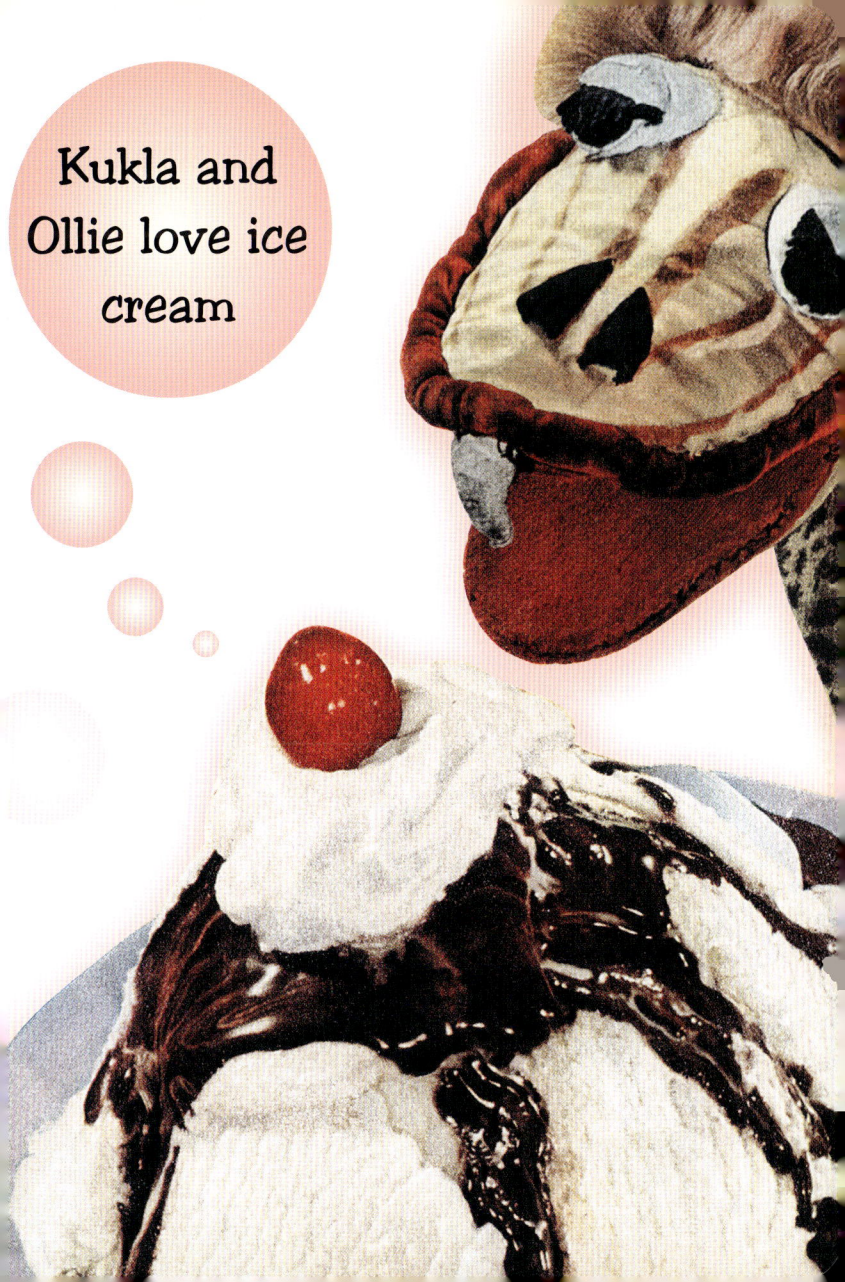

"Never eat more than your own weight in ice cream."

Miss Piggy

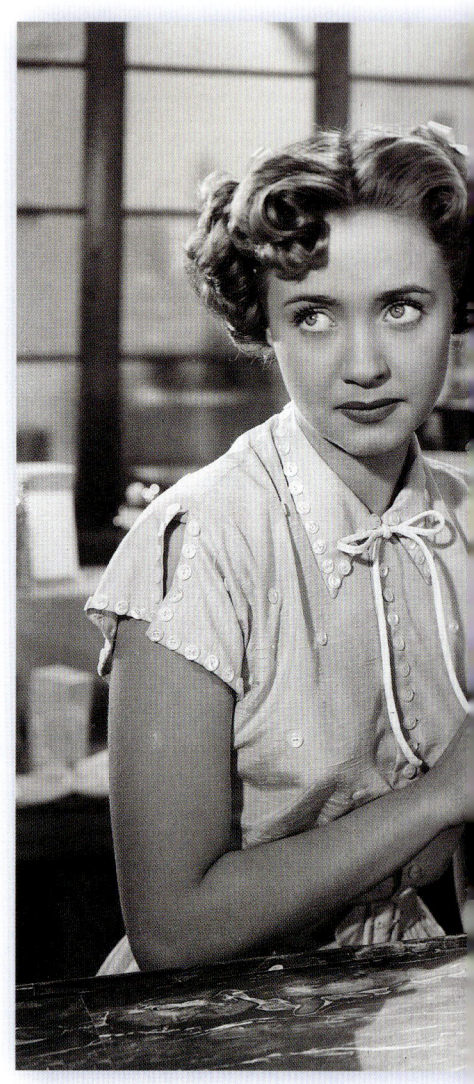

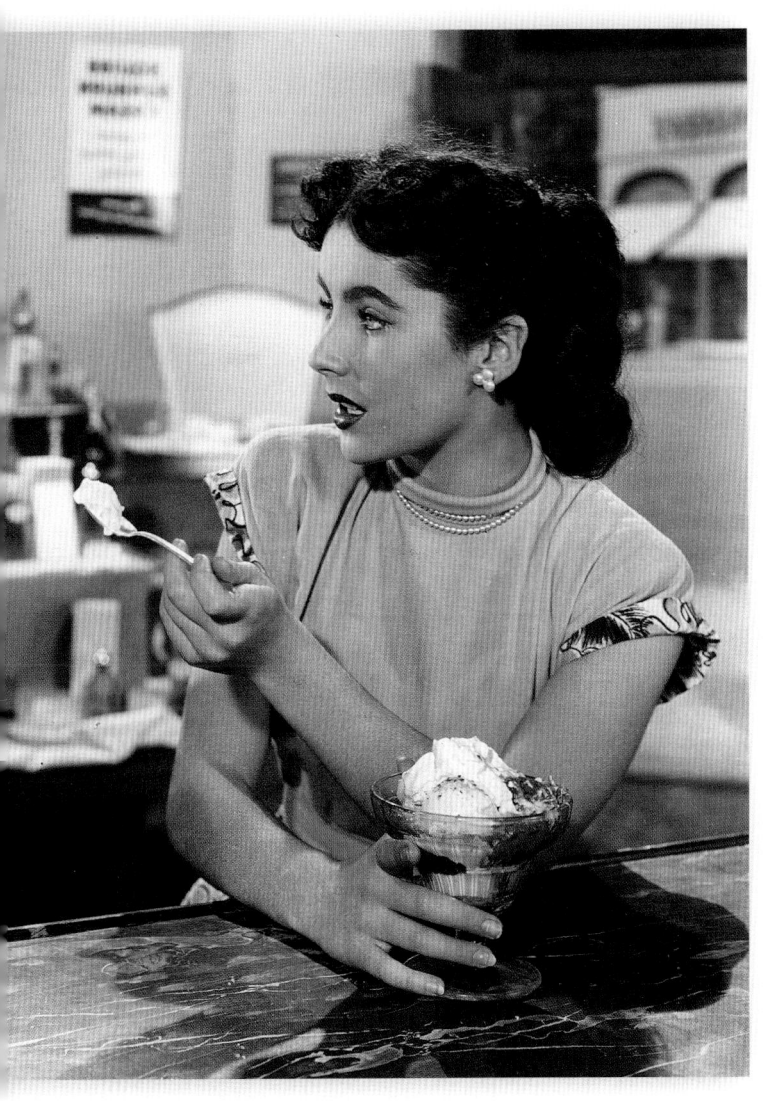

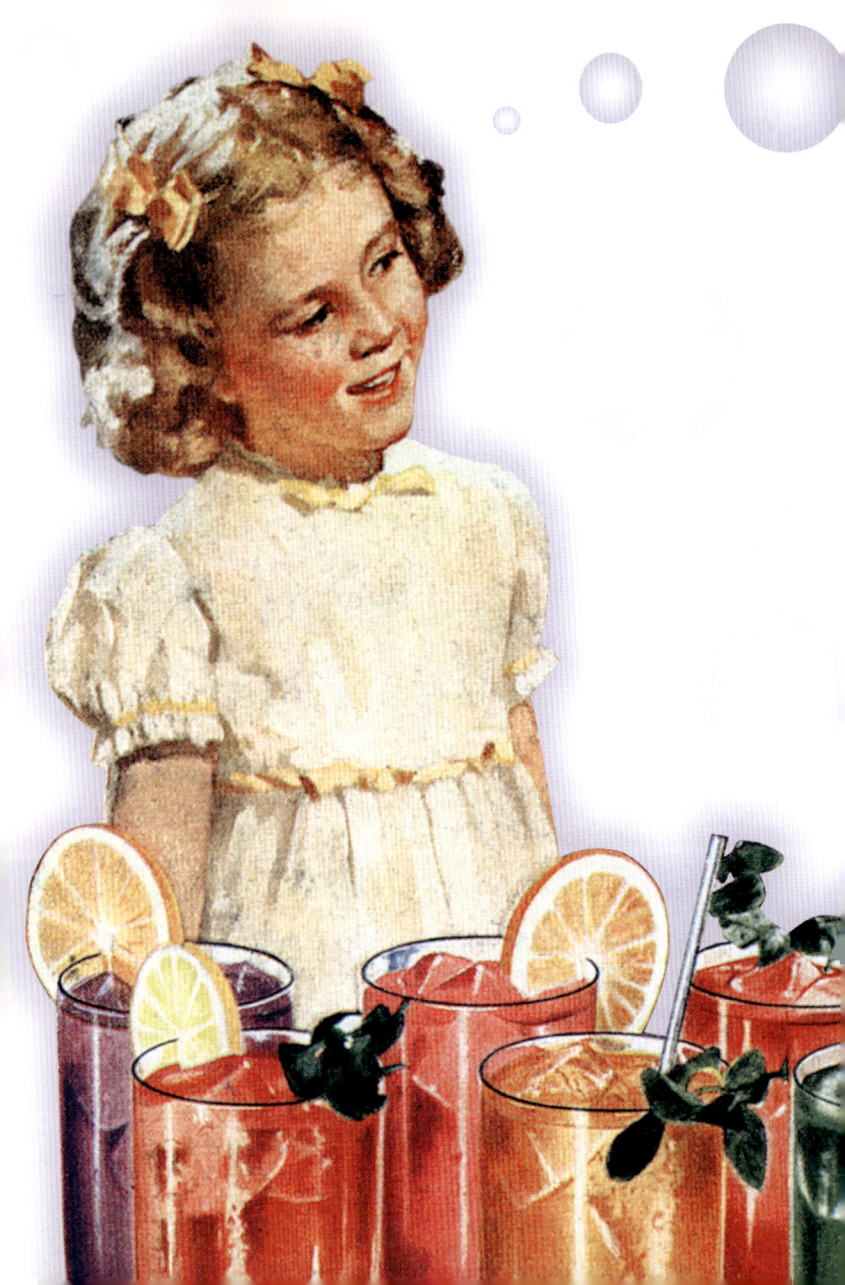

What bliss to perch on your seat at a friendly soda fountain and sip your favorite beverage through a straw! The fact is, it's just about impossible to be miserable when you're sipping a soda pop, flavored cola, float, or other fizzy concoction at the counter top. For generations, folks of all ages have flocked to the corner drugstore to enjoy magic moments of sweet refreshment. Originally, fizzy drinks such as phosphates, root beer, and ginger beer were based on homemade "pick-me-ups." Later, famous brands such as Coca-Cola came to the forefront. Soda fountains also had the approval of the temperance movement, which frowned on alcoholic drinks.

Chapter 3
SIPPIN' SODA

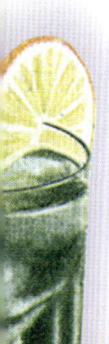

I've seen little things of eight and nine that had to be lifted up on the high stools at Eliot's drugstore, drinking great goblets of lemon soda, enough to burst them.

Stephen Leacock

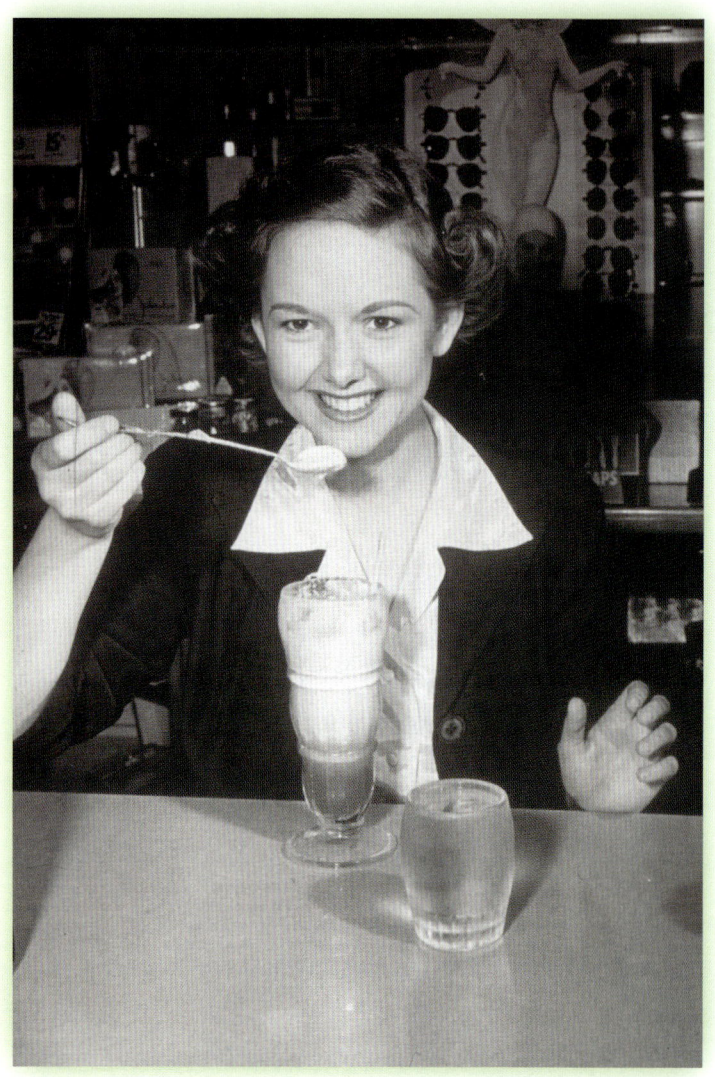

phosphates with fizz

Before there were bottles of Coke in every supermarket and store, there were soda fountains on every block where soda jerks would mix carbonated water with flavored syrups and talk to each other in a cryptic food language of illusions and symbols—"burn a crowd of van" (an order for three vanilla malteds) and "bucket of mud" (for a scoop of vanilla ice cream). Some of those syrups contained phosphoric acid, a tart flavor enhancer that also added fizz. In the new lingo, these sodas became known as phosphates.

James Beard Foundation

good for what ailed you

The first soda pops were based on early folk medicine recipes, and contained ingredients such as ginger, sarsaparilla, lemons, horseradish, nutmeg, sorrel, molasses, burdock, and dandelion. It's not clear who created the first soda—the issue is hotly contested. The first local brand to achieve national prominence in 1869 was Vernon's Ginger Ale. Afterward, scores of new sodas followed—in 1886 the first version of Coca-Cola appeared, also Dr. Pepper, and Hires Root Beer; then came Pepsi-Cola in 1898, Canada Dry Ginger Ale in 1904, and 7-UP in 1933.

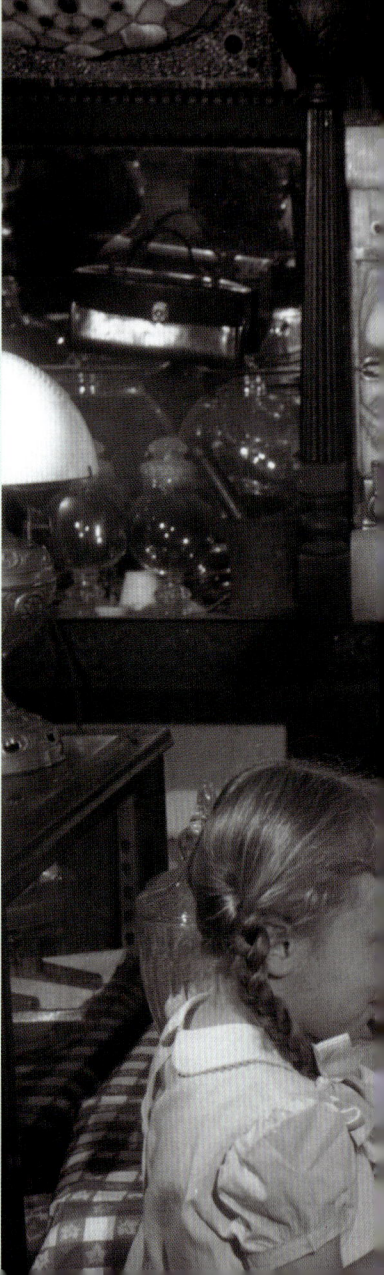

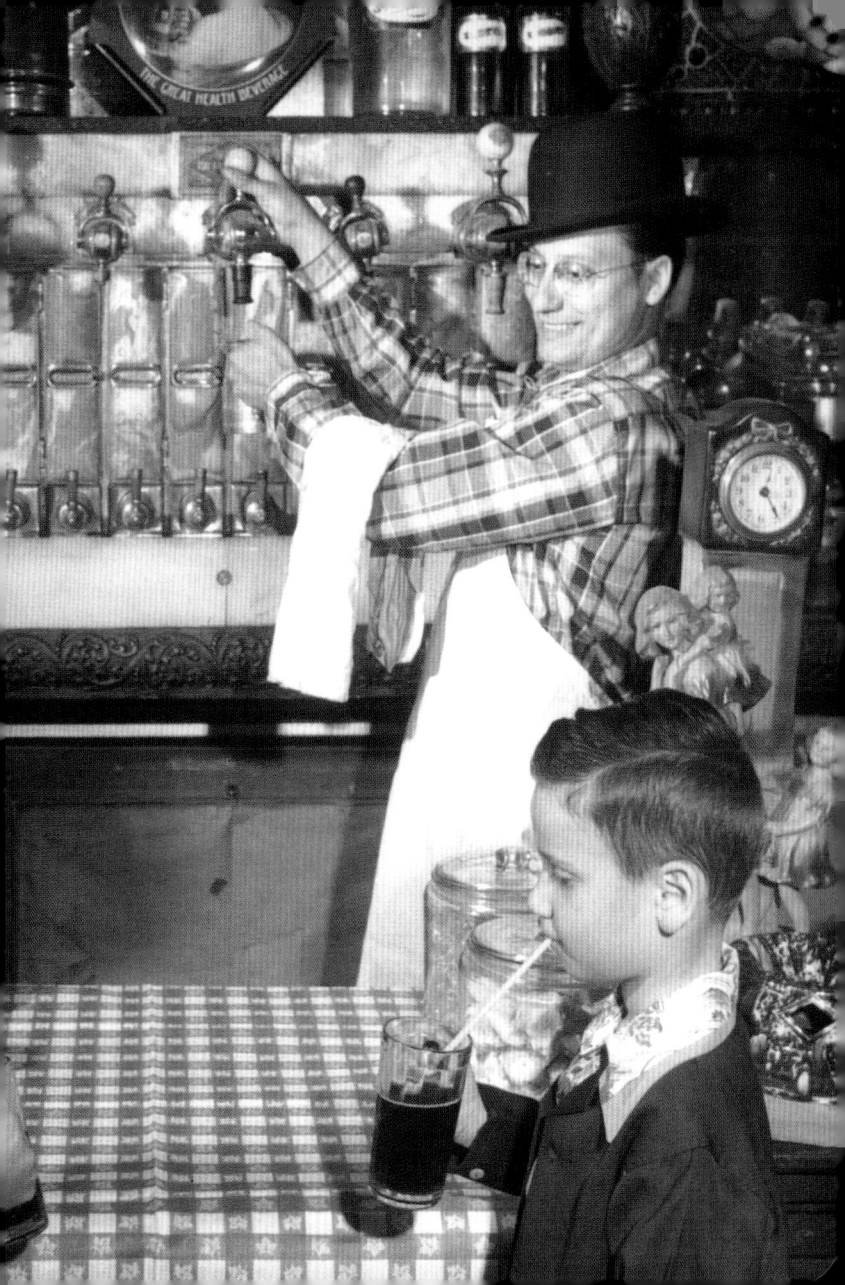

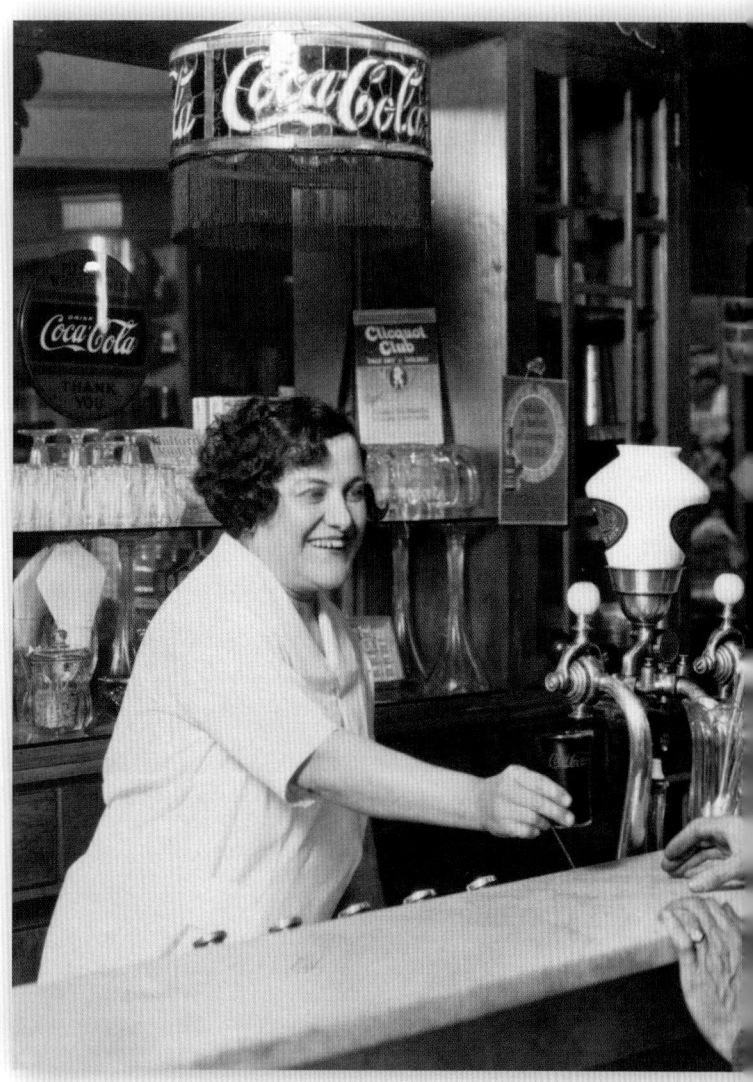

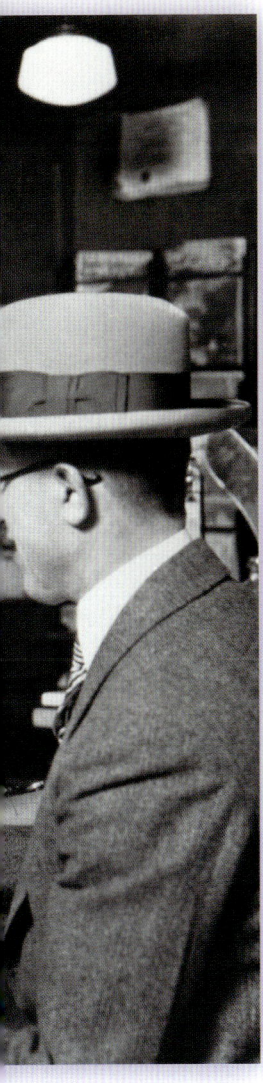

Coca-Cola rules

Ginger ale, "celerystone cola" and fruit-flavored phosphates were offered, but some soft drinks were intended as medicinal. The locally produced Thea Soda was touted to "clear the brain, steady the nerves, pick you up." Thea Soda had that in common with another offering, Pepsi-Cola, which had been created by a North Carolina druggist in the 1890s as an alternative to alcohol and as a medicine, to cure dyspepsia and peptic ulcers, hence its name. But Coca-Cola was king. Coca-Cola had been developed by John Pemberton, an Atlanta druggist, in 1886 as "the ideal nerve tonic and stimulant" that he hoped would supplant alcoholic beverages. The temperance movement latched onto the idea, and by 1905 Coca-Cola was marketed as "The Great National Temperance Drink."

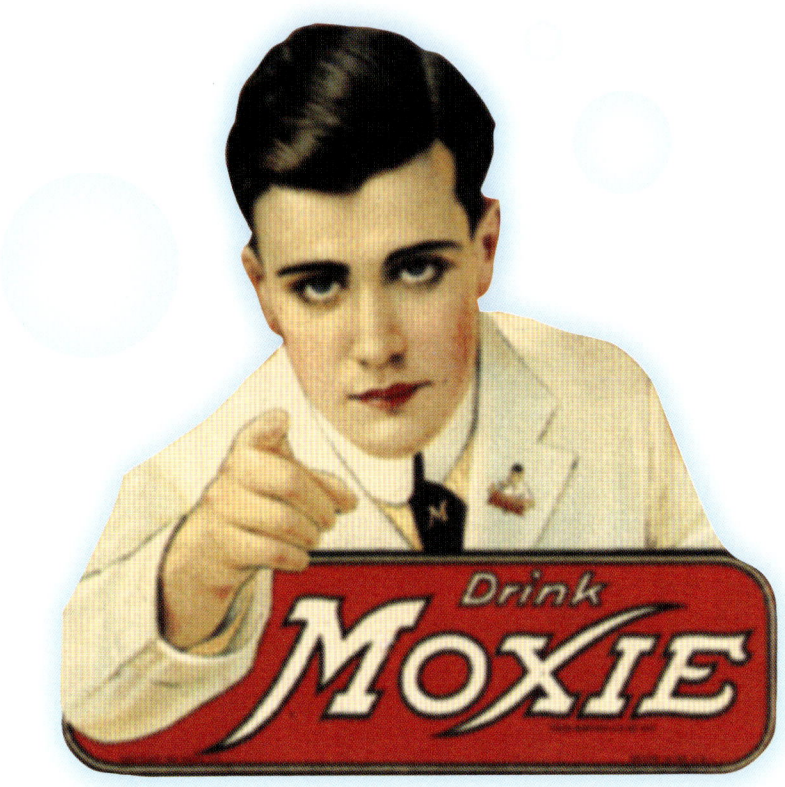

real Moxie!

Advertising was the key to success of the earliest sodas—and transformed them into familiar brand names. Moxie was a perfect example of creative marketing—by 1920, the company's sales of 25 million cases outdid even Coca-Cola.

The Moxie logo was printed on all kinds of items, from candy tins to Tiffany lamps. The company even had a special theme song published—"MOXIE, oh MOXIE, me for you, I don't know what I could do without you, As a drink you're a hummer in winter or summer...".

> "He sure has got a lotta Moxie!"

A huge surge in sugar prices in 1925 forced the company to cut back drastically, but Moxie is still often used as a word meaning "courage" or "spirit."

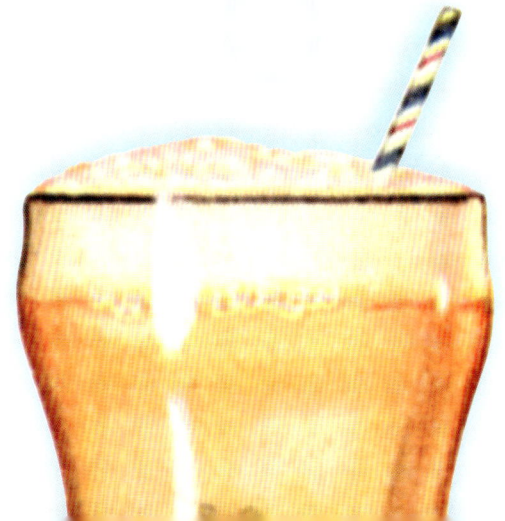

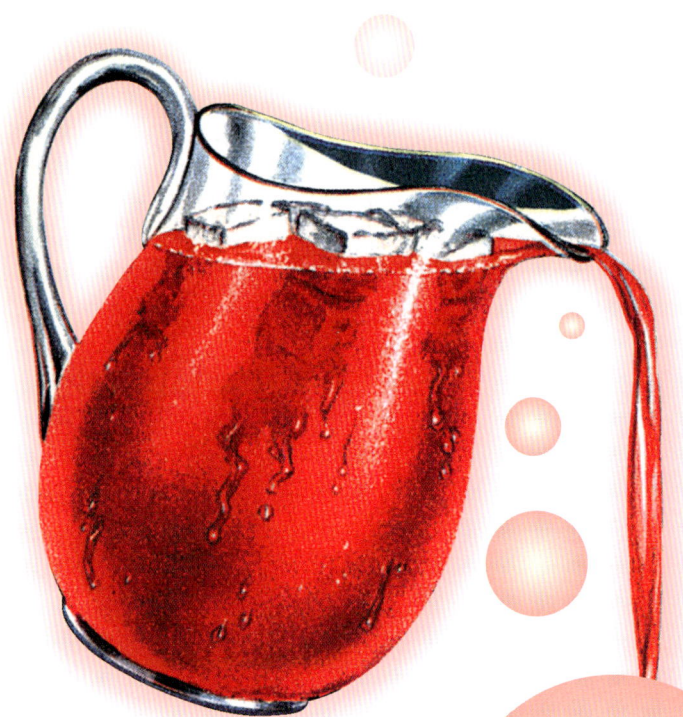

2 tbsp. of strawberry syrup or flavoring
seltzer water as required
1 large scoop of very hard vanilla ice cream

Strawberry Soda

(In the Hay)

1 Put the flavoring in the bottom of a large soda glass.

2 Add seltzer water to within 2 inches (5 cm.) of the lip of the glass, stirring as you pour.

3 Add the ice cream, keeping it even with the rim of the glass, but submerged enough so that it reacts with the seltzer to create a foamy head. If the ice cream is too deep in the seltzer, the soda will overflow. If it isn't deep enough, you don't have a soda. With practice, you'll reach a perfect balance.

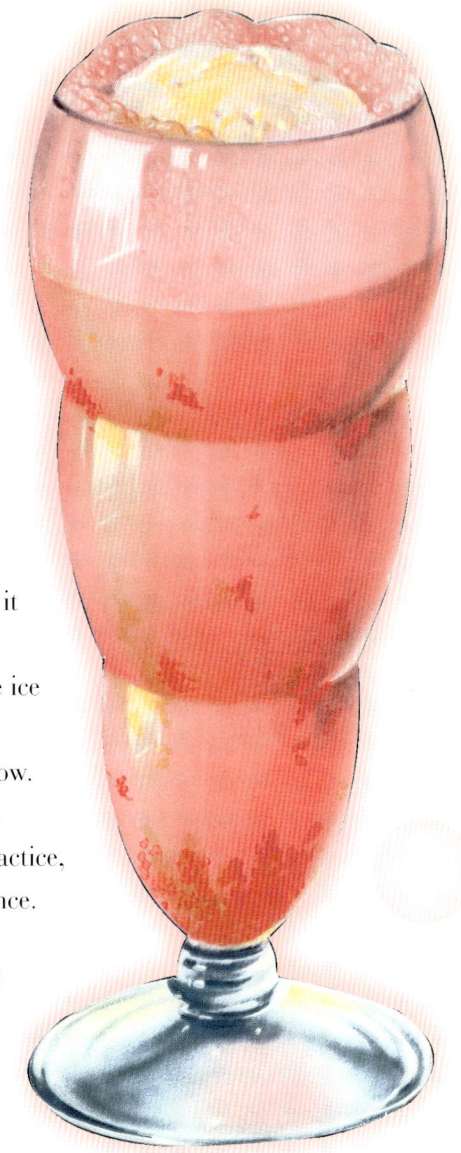

cheap and cheerful too!

My favorite drinks are soda fountain colas. Cherry Coke, vanilla Coke, chocolate Coke—I love them all. As a kid in Highland, Ilinois, my friends and I would order cherry Cokes at our local Rexall Drug Store whenever we had some spare change. We also liked the flavored Cokes because they were one of the cheaper drinks we could order. Cash was always in short supply at that age. If I was really flush, I'd get a strawberry soda which had ice cream in it.

Dan Stieb

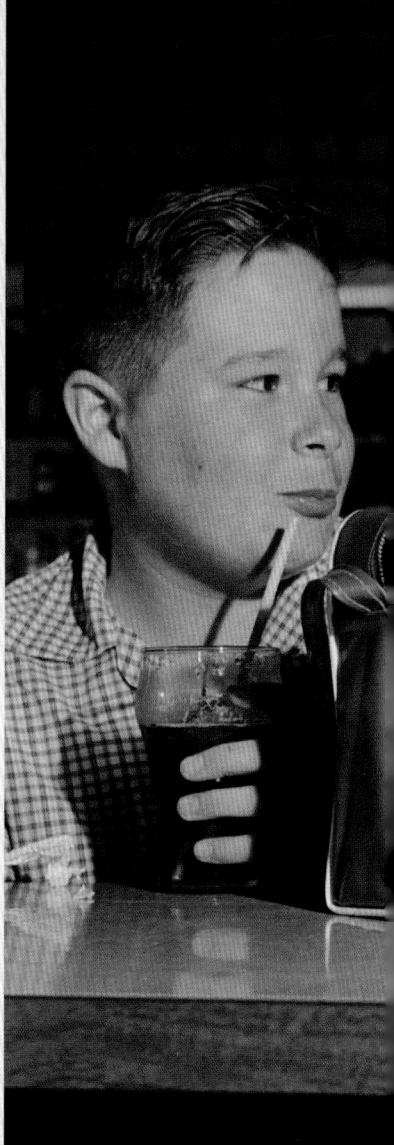

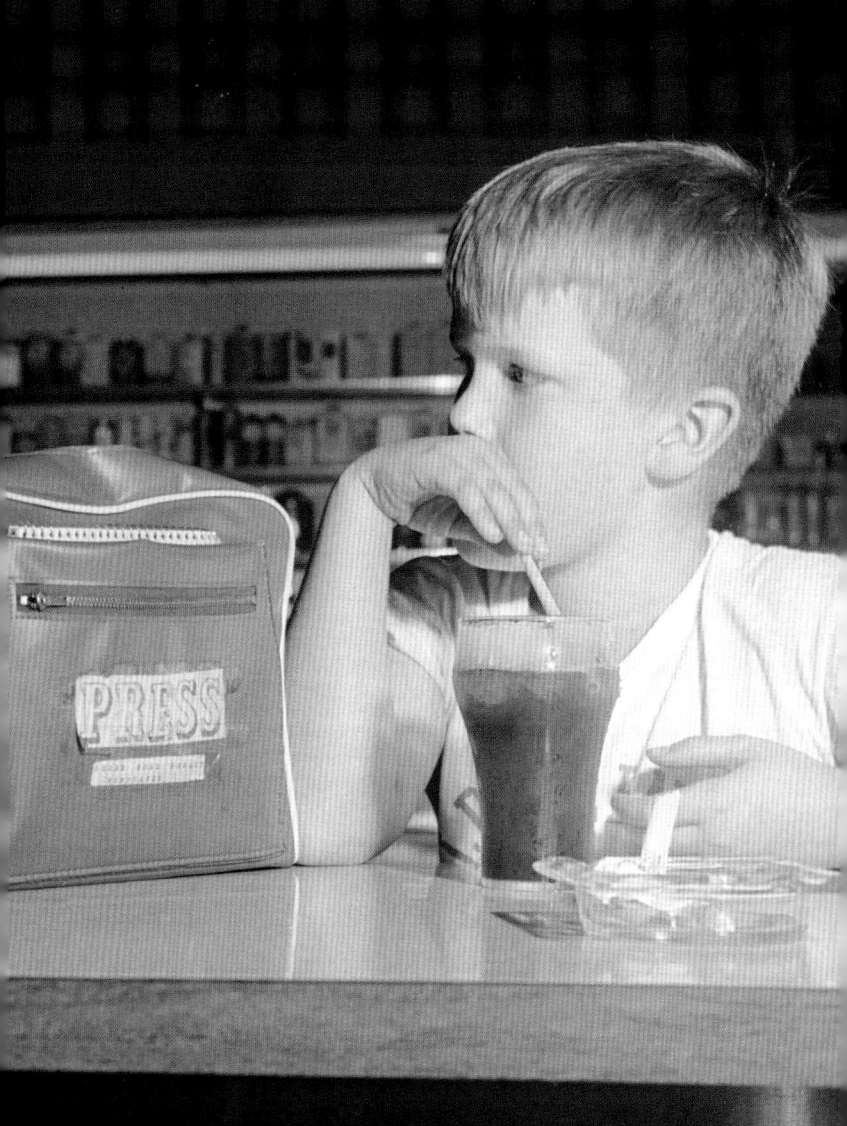

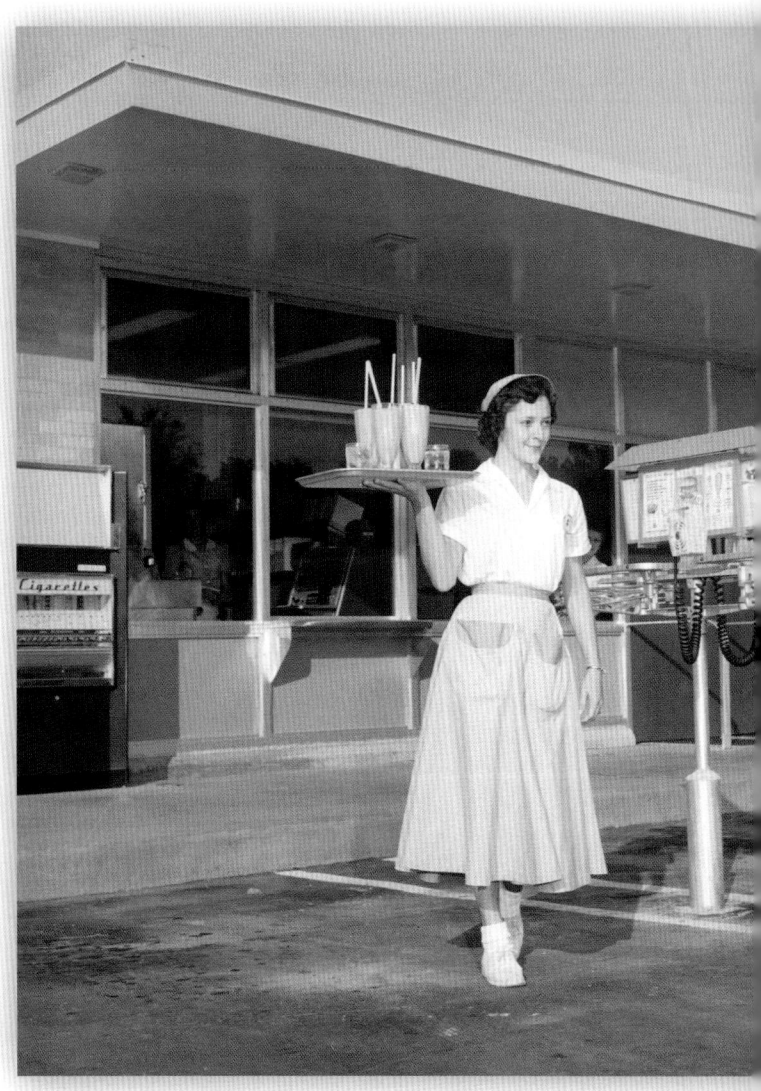

curb service

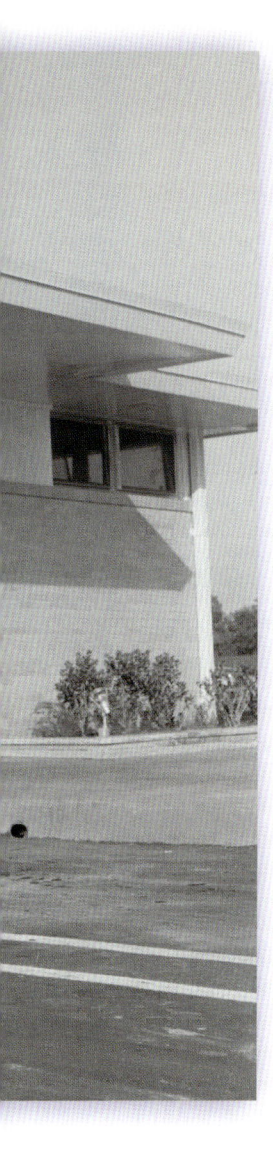

My favorite stop was the A&W root beer stand, on Woodlawn and Central, about two miles north and a mile east of the Dairy Queen and King's X. By then we had a 1956 Buick Super, with a V-8 engine, air conditioning, four doors, and an automatic transmission. Girls would bring out food and drinks on a silvery metal tray with a leg that fit onto a partially rolled-up window. When we first went, it was just for the ice-cold, steaming cold, frosted mugs that said "A&W" on them. That root beer had a creamy head and a fulfilling sweetness you can't get now with all the high fructose corn syrup in everything. It really cooled and refreshed.

Rod Owen

an old-fashioned chocolate malt

4 scoops vanilla ice cream
1 1/2 cups (375 ml.) milk
2 to 3 tbsp. chocolate syrup
1 tsp. vanilla extract
2 tbsp. malted milk powder

1 Blend everything until no white is showing.

2 Serve immediately with a dollop of whipped cream.

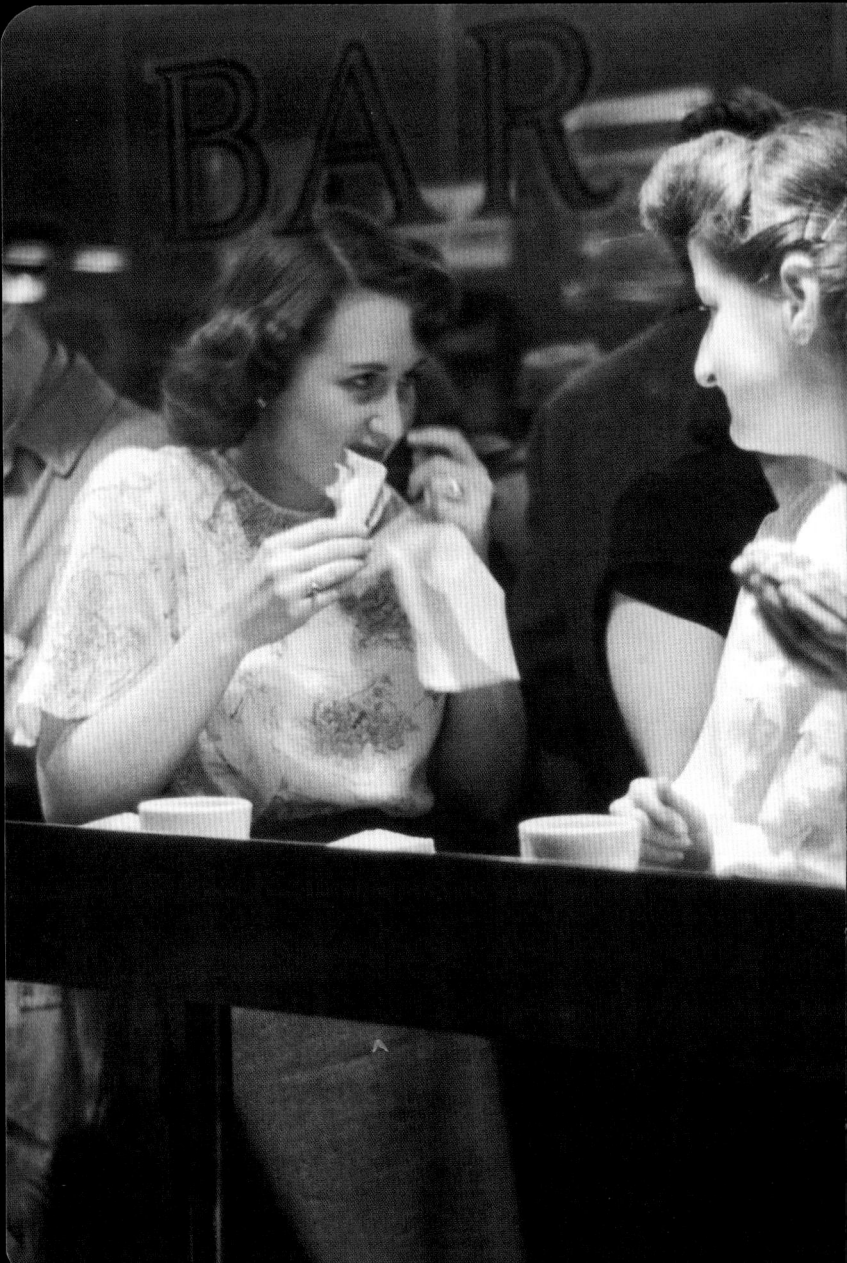

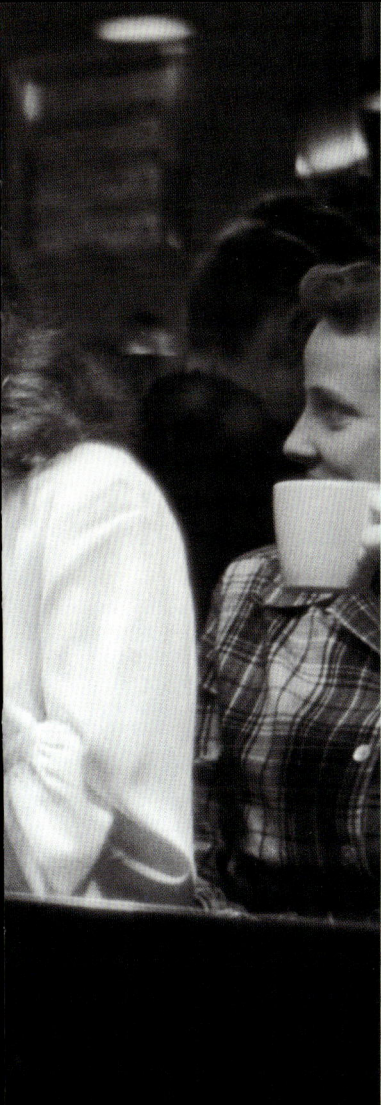

New York's special treat

Home is where the heart is, and for me it is Brooklyn. Original home of the Brooklyn Dodgers (dem bums). But what defined the imagination of a soda jerk and the customer was the all-famous EGG CREAM. This was a concoction of chocolate syrup, milk, and seltzer, which had neither an egg nor cream in it. But for us Brooklynites, a candy store minus an egg cream was as inconceivable as a kitchen table without an oilcloth.

Phyllis Prussick

plop! fizz! fizz!

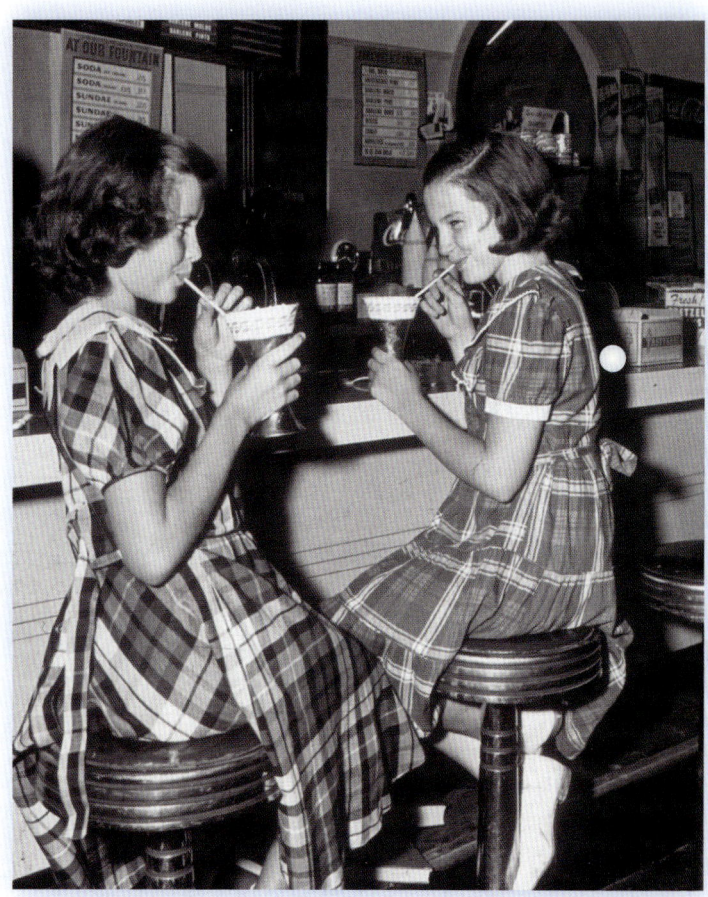

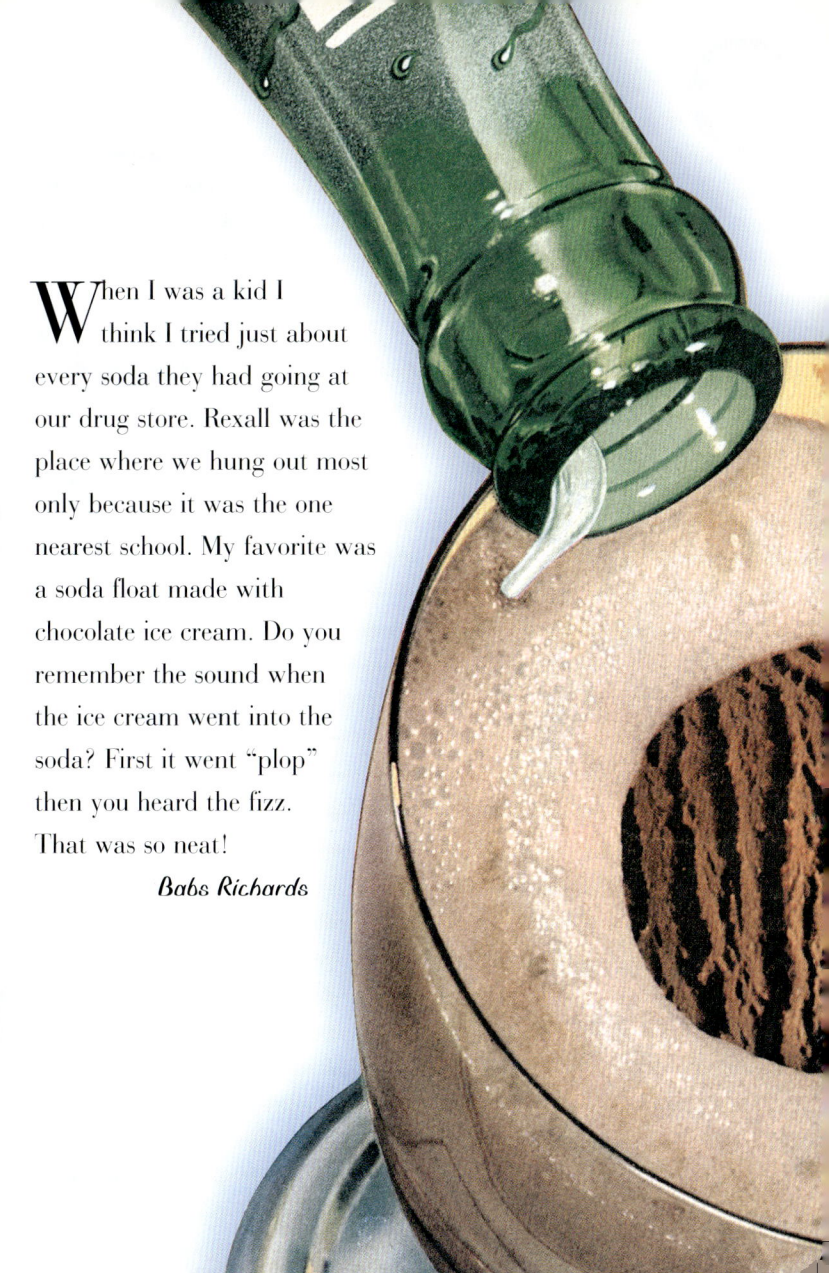

When I was a kid I think I tried just about every soda they had going at our drug store. Rexall was the place where we hung out most only because it was the one nearest school. My favorite was a soda float made with chocolate ice cream. Do you remember the sound when the ice cream went into the soda? First it went "plop" then you heard the fizz. That was so neat!

Babs Richards

It's the little things in life that make such a big difference. That welcoming "hello" from the owner of the soda fountain; the fact that the soda jerk always remembered your favorite treat, and took care to fix it just the way you liked it; the encouraging word for youngsters struggling with schoolwork— all these small kindnesses created a benign feeling that there was time for everyone, young and old.

Chapter 4
TREAT ME NICE

Of neighborhoods, benevolence is the most beautiful. How can the man be considered wise who, when he had the choice, does not settle in benevolence.

Confucius

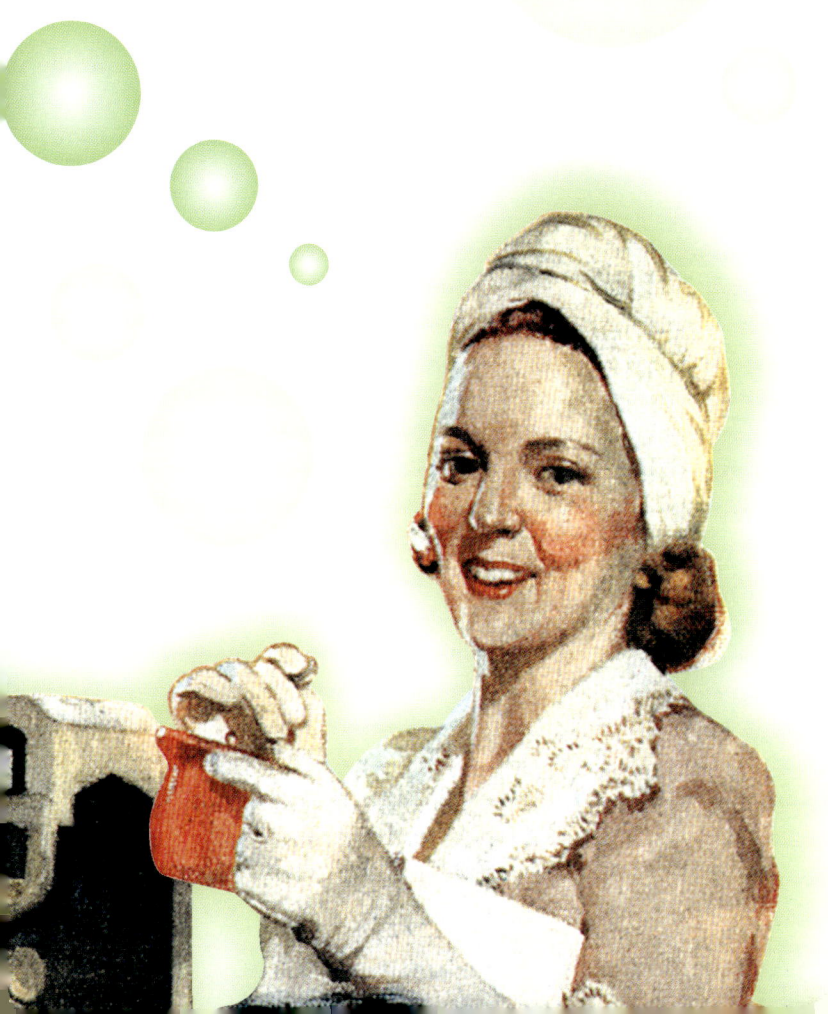

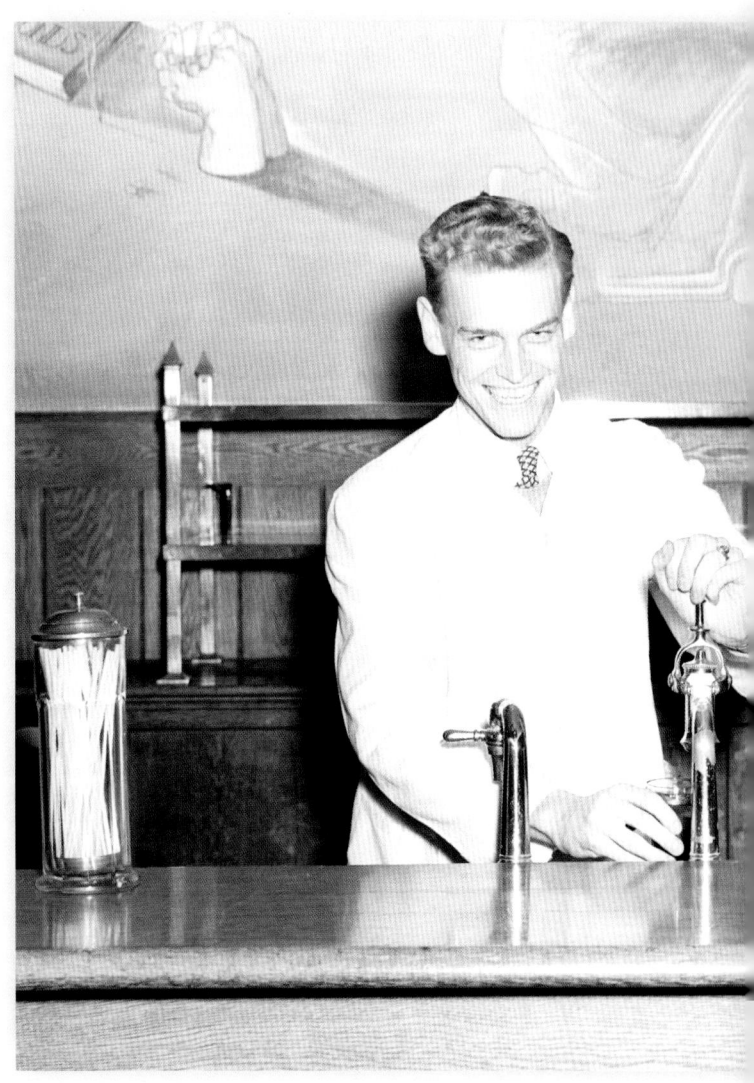

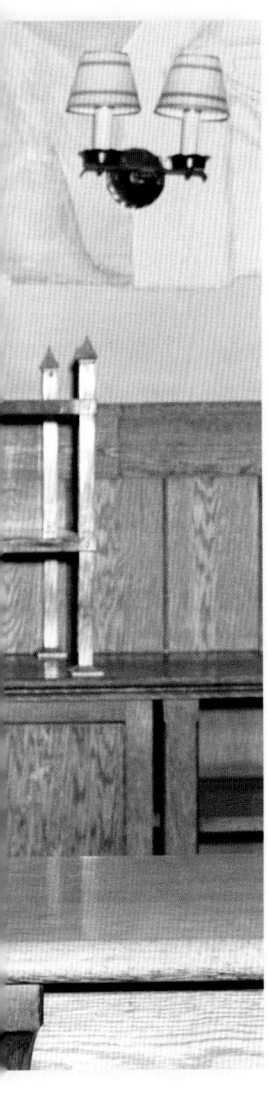

oh! so cool

Soda fountains bring back warm memories of good times and frosty concoctions. Fountains had their heyday from about the 1920s until the 1950s.

Soda jerks clerked at these hot spots. They earned their name from jerking fountain handles forward to draw soda water into a mug. Shining with marble, metal, and glass, the numerous spigots and taps spewed forth carbonated water, ice cream, and syrup. Soda jerks mixed such frothy brews as strawberry floats, cherry Cokes, banana splits, double chocolate malts, and black-and-white sodas. During the twenties, refrigeration allowed operators to serve entire meals, not just ice cream and other snacks. Therefore, fountains popped up in many department stores, five-and-tens, luncheonettes, and groceries.

Glenn Emery

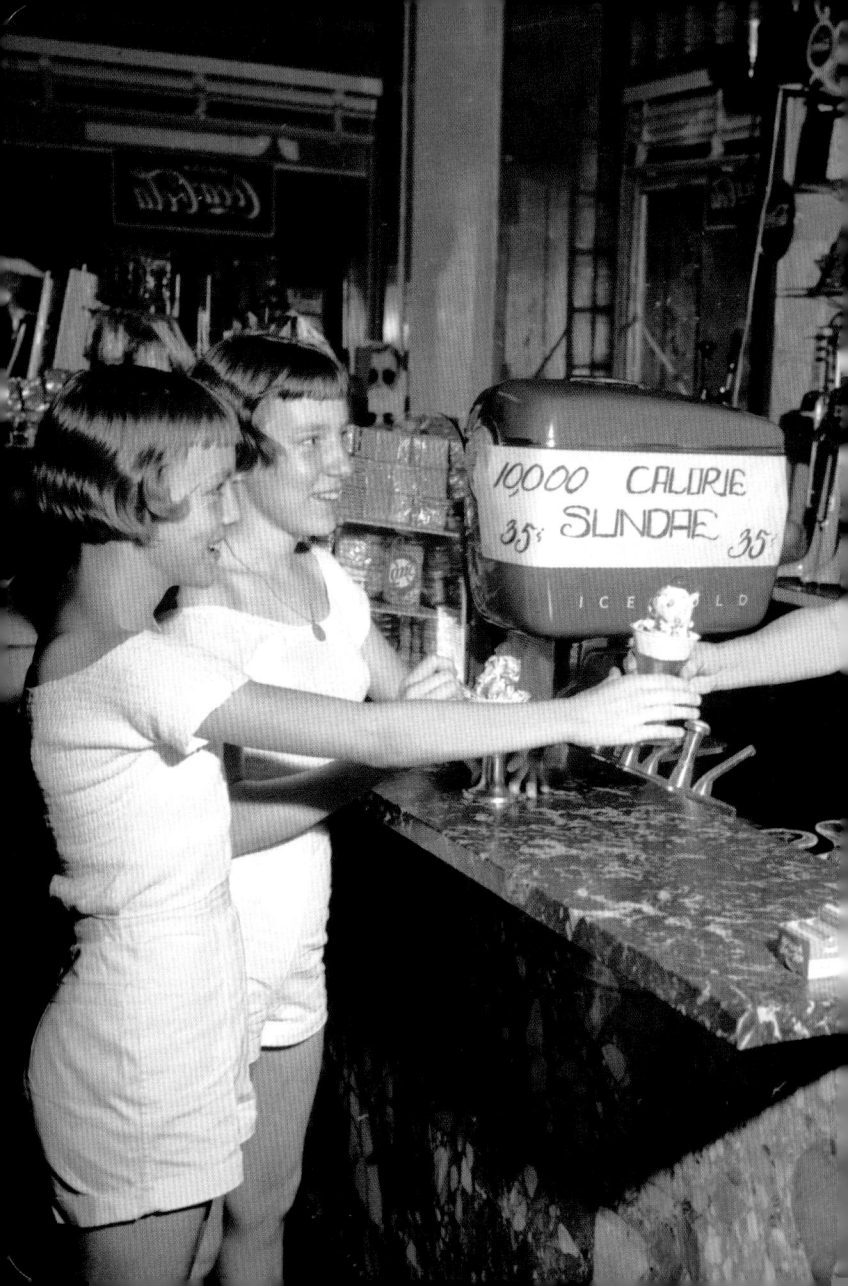

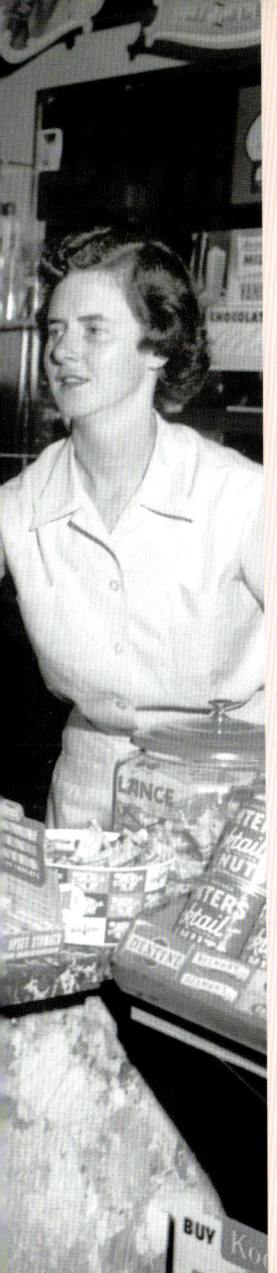

an encouraging word for all

I was such a regular at our soda fountain that the owner, Mrs Simmons, used to laugh and ask me when I was planning to move in. That was after I asked if I could get a job there as a soda jerk when I left school. She said that maybe ten years old was too young to decide, but she'd think about it. She always asked me what we were studying at school, and how I was doing. Her favorite subject was history—she knew all sorts of stuff—and when I showed her my report card, she gave me a banana split for free if I'd got a good grade. Looking back, I think she was one of those people who are naturally bright and interested in everything, and that's why she always had an encouraging word for all us kids.

Mike Long

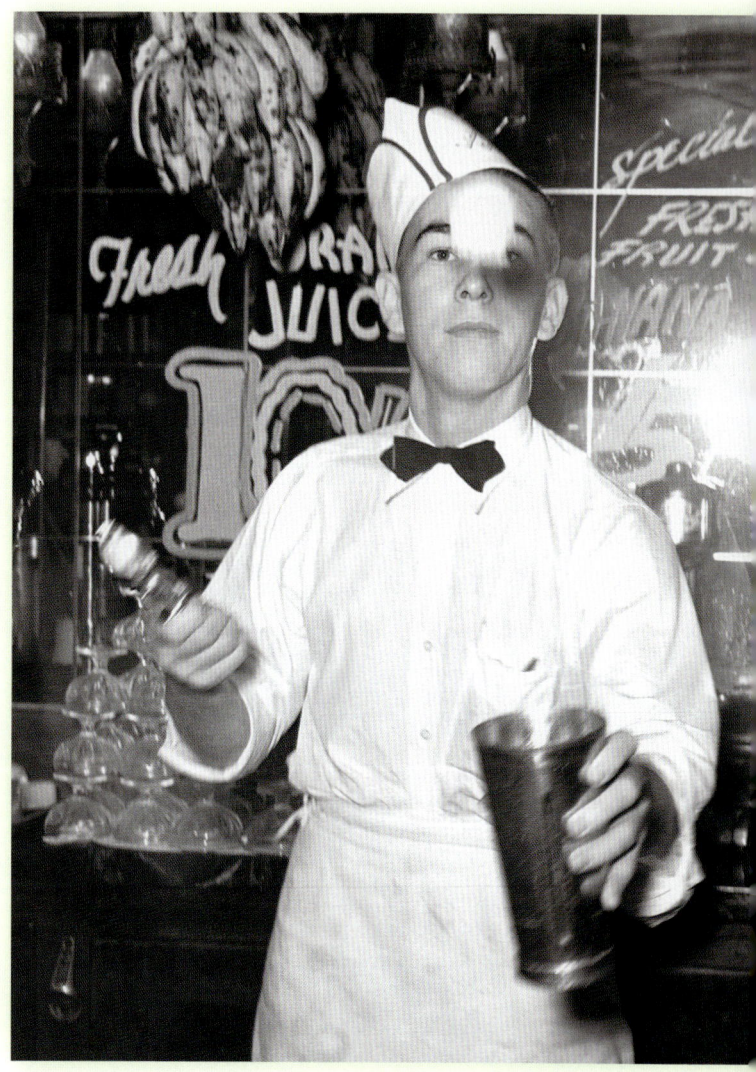

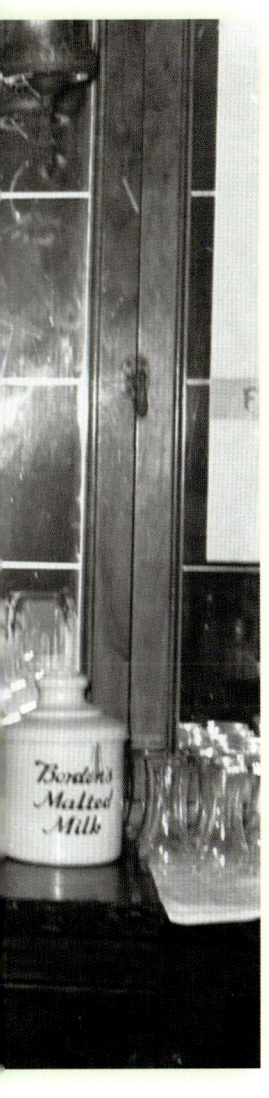

served with a flourish

Every pharmacy and five-and-ten used to have a counter employing virtual architects of sundaes and ice cream sodas. These confectionery choreographers often had such refined technique that they were able to fill their vessels to that magical level just over the brim. To top it off, these creations were invariably served with a flourish and the grace of a dancer.

By the time of my childhood, these counters were usually "manned" by teenage girls or older women in white uniforms. A few ancient drugstores still managed to field a soda jerk, or "fountain professional." This almost always seemed to be a semi-retired man or teenage boy who looked positively military in crisp white trousers, short white jacket and, of course, the white overseas cap.

Peter Dervis

People didn't like the term soda jerk, so we started calling ourselves FIZZicians and fountainers. We had a lot of fun. We opened at seven in the morning and closed at ten, except on Saturday nights when we closed at ten-thirty after the preview movie got out. They would fill this place up. I've always had a soft place in my heart for fountains all my life because that's where I got my start before I went to college to become a pharmacist.

Kenneth Eck

we say FIZZicians

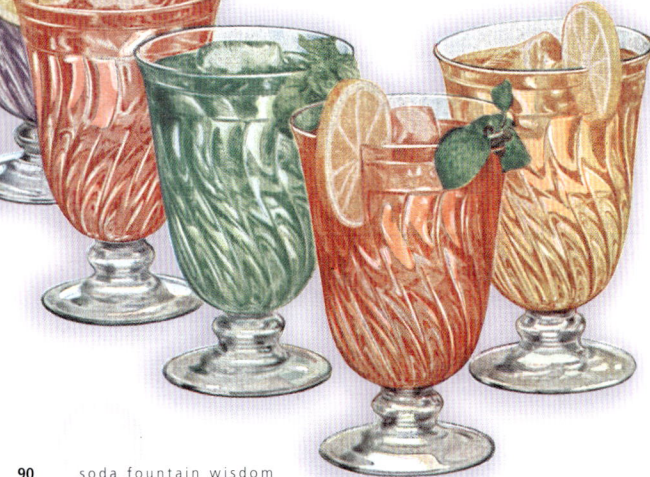

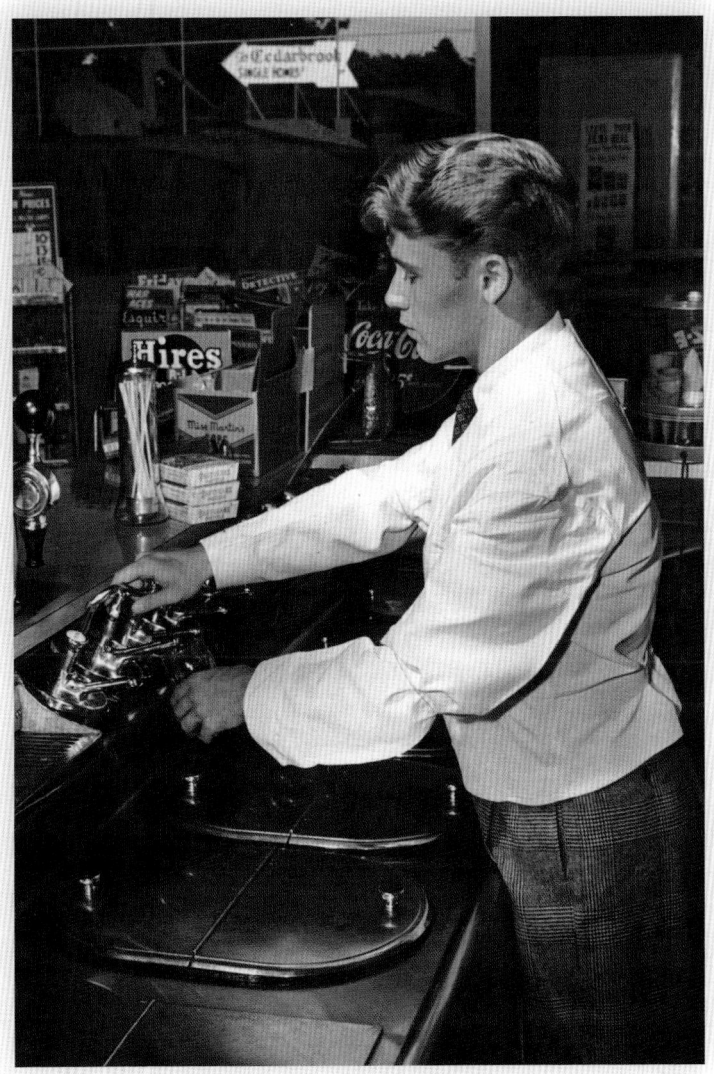

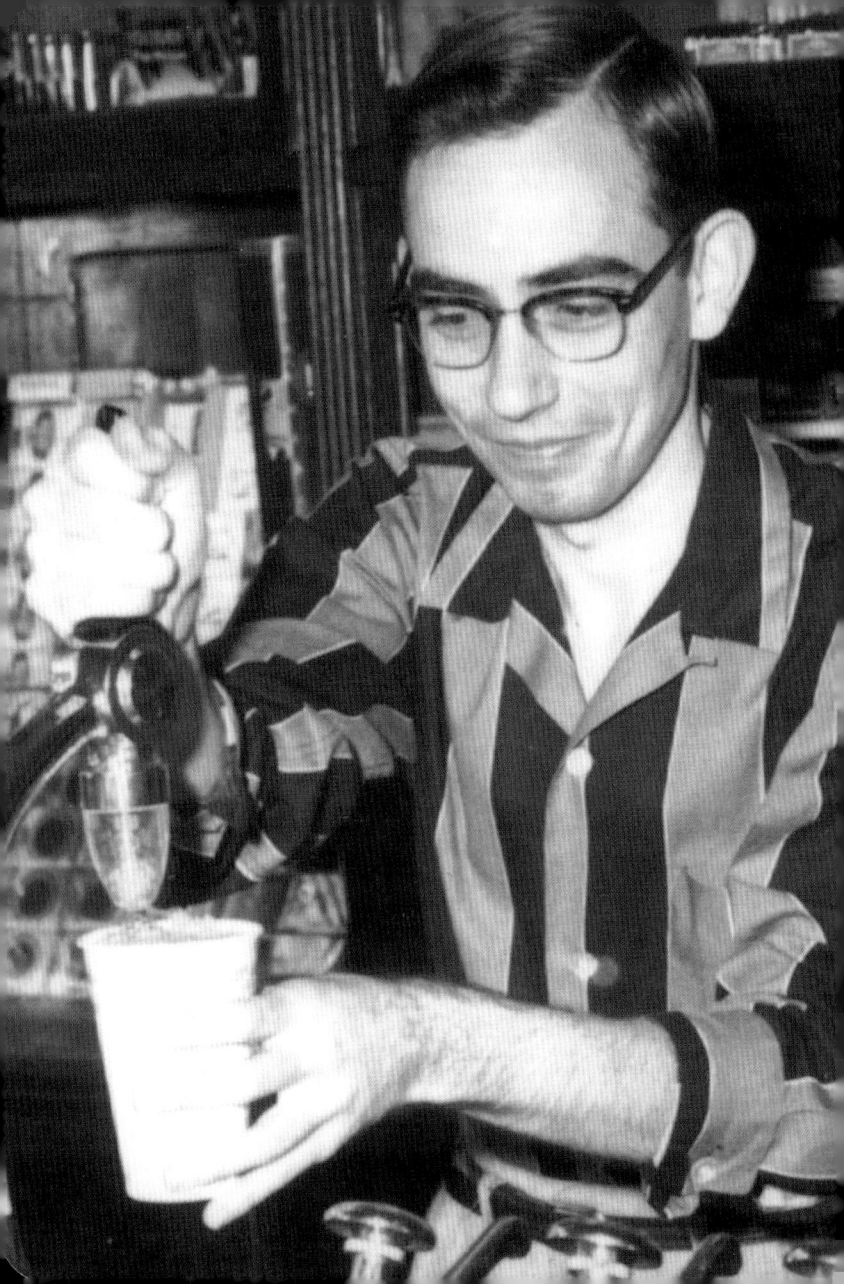

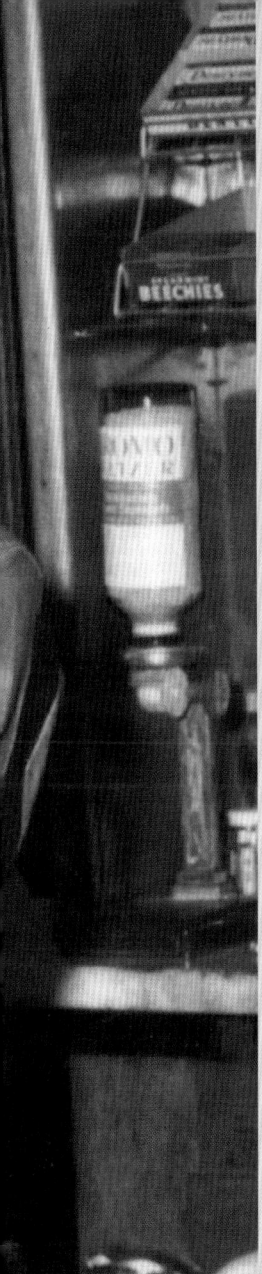

job of a lifetime

I've been the soda jerk at Hunter Drug, Greensburg, Kansas, for over fifty years.

I often mixed up Bromo-Seltzer for people. There was a train engineer who was terribly fond of these who came in regularly. The bad thing was his skin was starting to look a little blue from the bromo.

We never served sandwiches, only drinks and ice cream. But I've always made "special drinks" for people. I'll make small sodas or small 400's (a 400 is milk with flavoring and a little ice). I usually just make 12-oz. glasses of those but I'll make 6 oz. if someone really wants one. People always want me to wait on them—they say the drink just doesn't taste right unless Dick makes it! I can remember people that came in the store once, two years ago. I always like to make the customer feel special.

Richard Huckriede

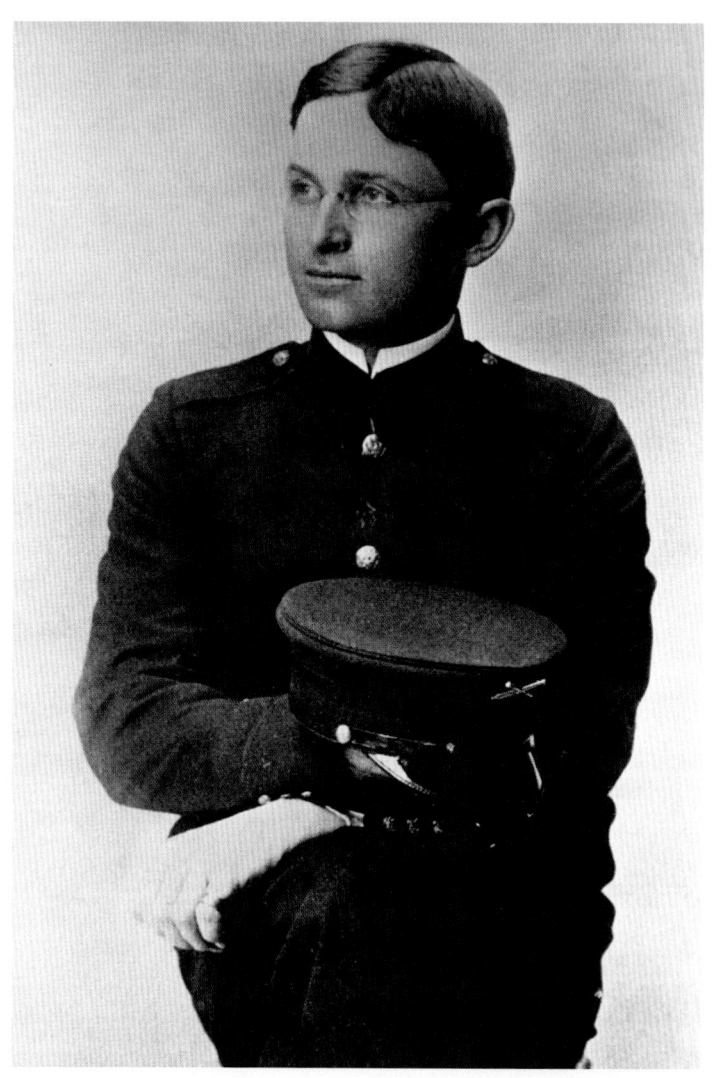

Harry Truman's first job

"I can remember the first $3.00 I received for working a week. It was in Jim Clinton's drugstore; I had to wipe off the bottles, mop the floor every morning, make ice cream for sodas, and wait on the customers. That three silver dollars looked like three million and meant a lot more. I've never had as much or as big a payday since."

Harry S. Truman

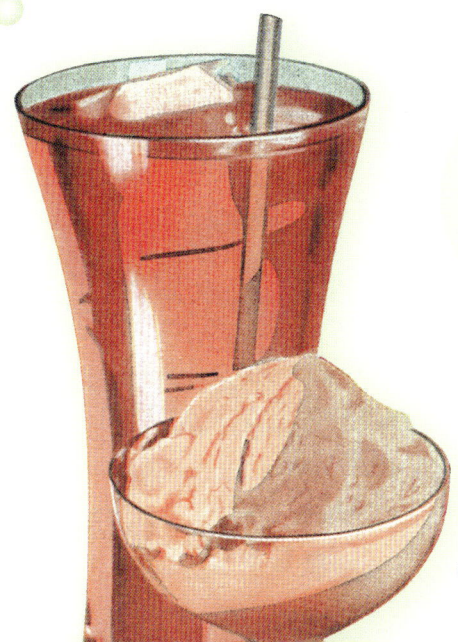

treat me nice

soda jerk's lingo

Soda jerks are inventive in all kinds of ways! Here are some special code names for soda fountain drinks:

- 91: one water, 92: two waters

- 200: small chocolate milk

- 400: large chocolate milk

- Shoot one: Coke

- Shoot one muddy: chocolate Coke

- Shoot one wild: cherry Coke

- Shoot one sour: lime Coke

- Wacko in Dixie: Dr. Pepper in a paper cup

- Anything walking: To go

- Brown/black cow: root beer soda

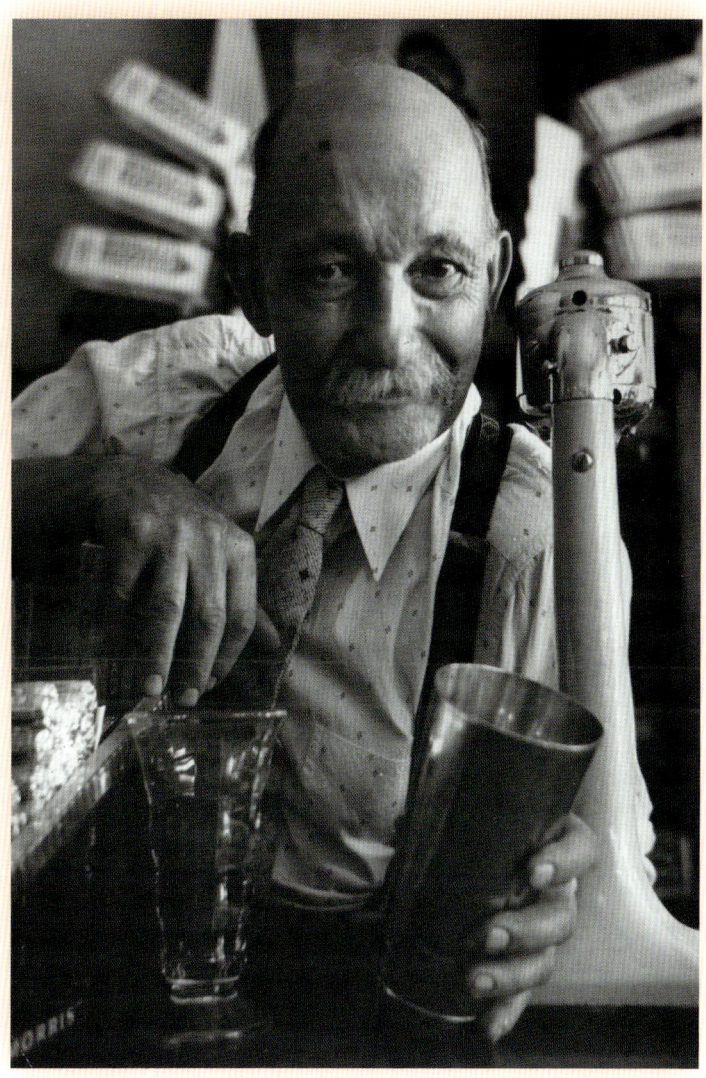

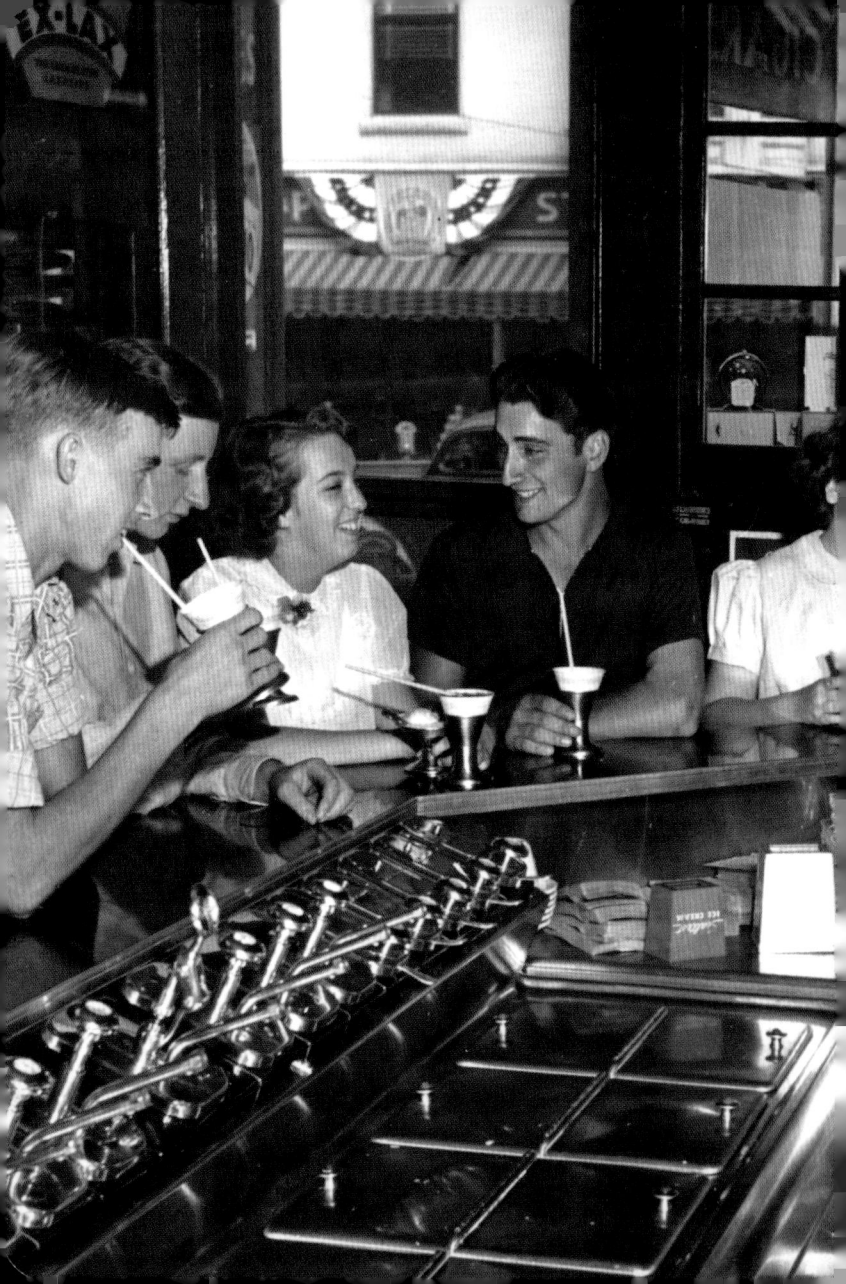

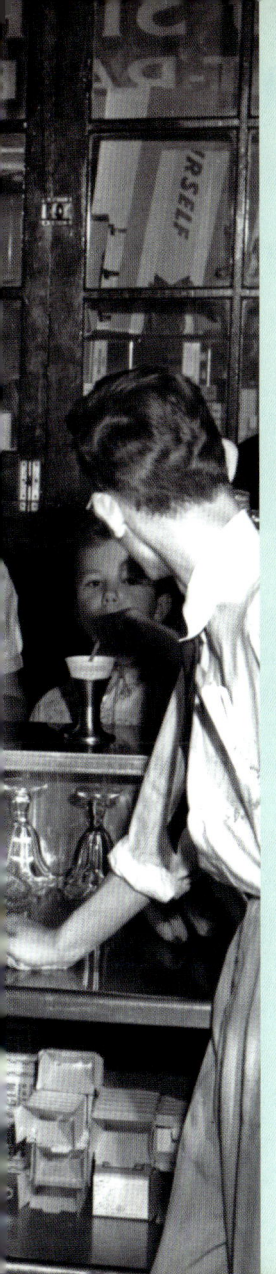

soda fountain calls

It's a classic moment from one of those old television shows or movies. The customer walks into a diner and chooses something to eat—let's say it's a ham sandwich. The waitress then yells out to the cook "Dress one pig." This is an example of a coded "call"—a tradition that started in soda fountains, and later moved on to diners.

The famous American preacher and orator Henry Ward Beecher (1813-1887) was fascinated by these soda fountain calls. He enjoyed listening to the ingenious banter of the soda dispensers, and decided that he would test out the versatility of one in particular. So, he casually ordered two eggs on toast. The soda jerk automatically called out to the cook "Adam and Eve on a raft." Mr. Beecher then quickly asked to have the eggs scrambled. Without a moment's hesitation, the soda jerk shouted "and wreck'em."

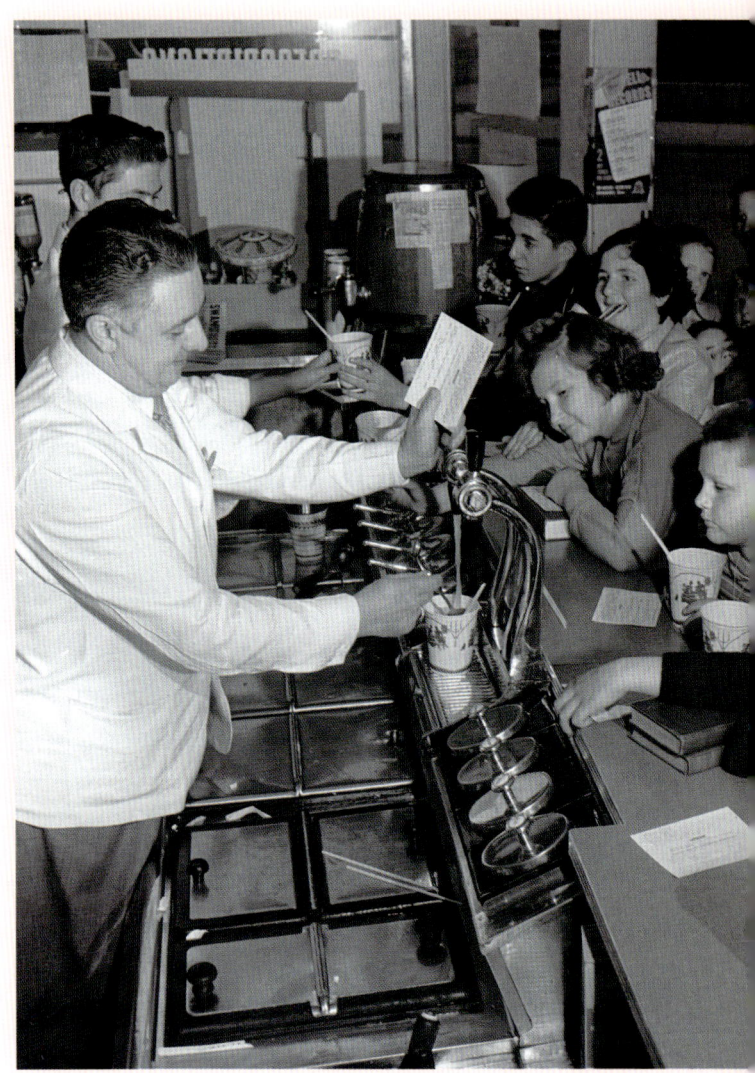

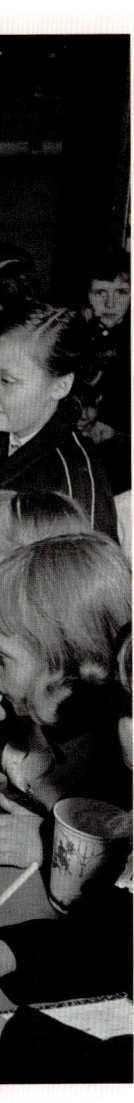

making the grade

Did you ever get any of those free soda deals? I remember they had them in the early 1950s. The way it worked was, you had to take your report card over to the soda fountain (I don't know how the people there got involved). Anyway, if your grades were good enough, you got a free soda. Everyone from my school stood in line at the counter, just hoping and hoping they would be OK for the free offer. I don't know whether I can say it really improved my grades though.

Joel White

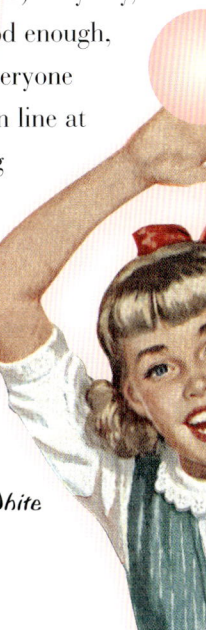

Chapter 5
DEVOTED TO YOU

The local soda fountain was the setting for all kinds of human dramas. It might be a young couple falling in love over a soda; shy college kids out on a first date; the high school team celebrating a football win; or old friends sharing problems and advice. If you stayed around long enough, romance, humor, hope, despair. and wise words would all come your way.

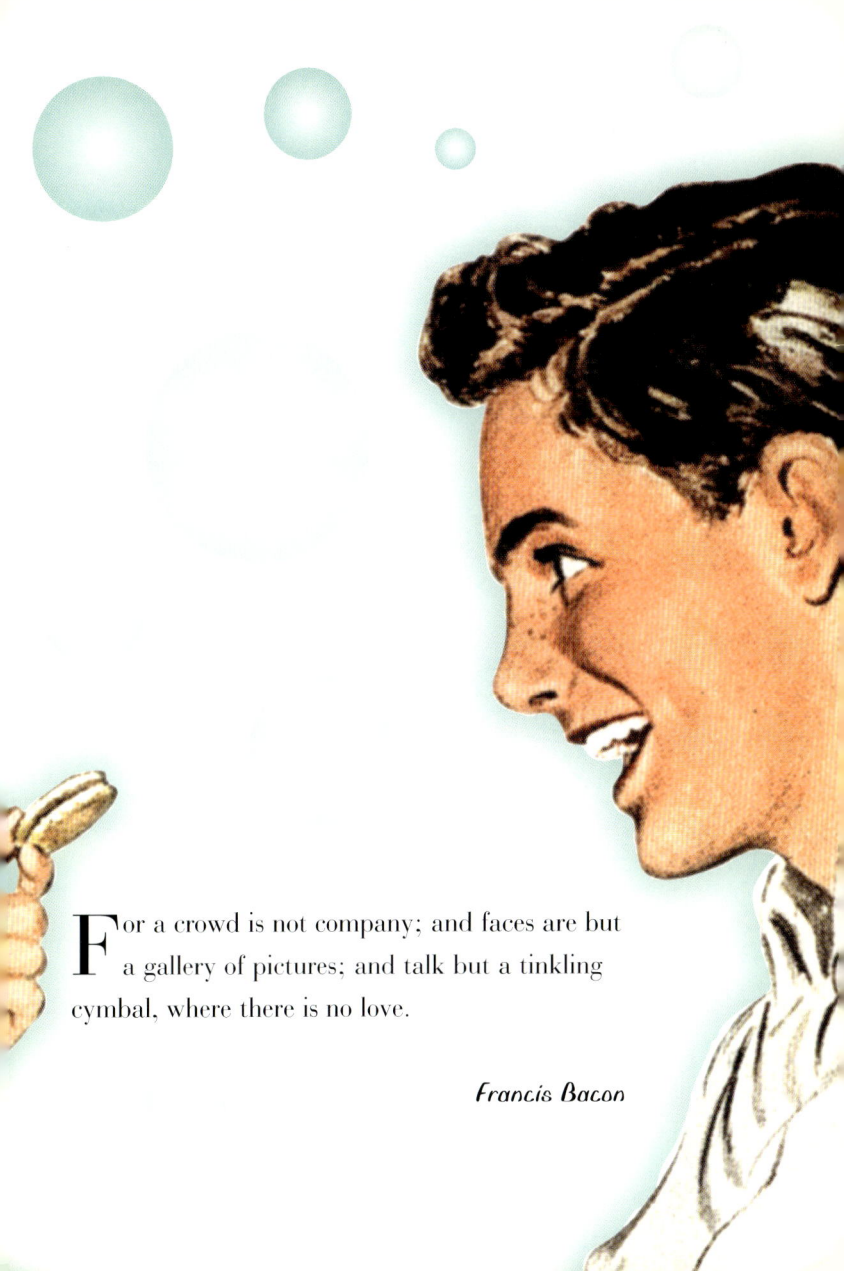

For a crowd is not company; and faces are but a gallery of pictures; and talk but a tinkling cymbal, where there is no love.

Francis Bacon

drugstore cowboys

By 3:15 p.m. the place was a den of noise, filled with unending chatter about what was going on at school, who was dating whom, which romances were beginning or ending, who was getting a driver's license, or how badly we would beat our opponents in the next ball game. My seventh and eighth grade teacher, Miss Edith Holt, one day laughingly tagged those of us who "hung out" at Flippin's in the afternoons as "Drugstore Cowboys."

Don Harold Lawrence

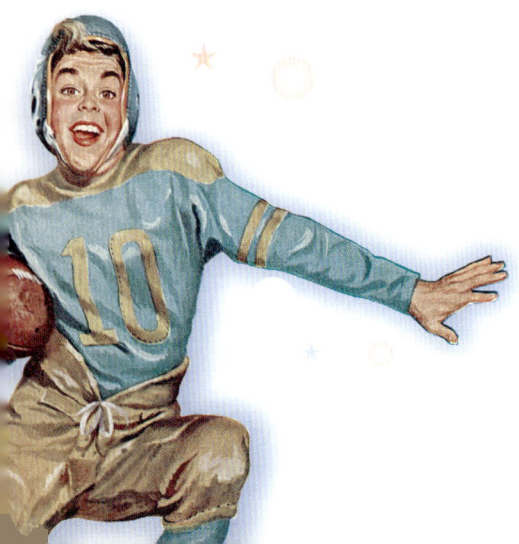

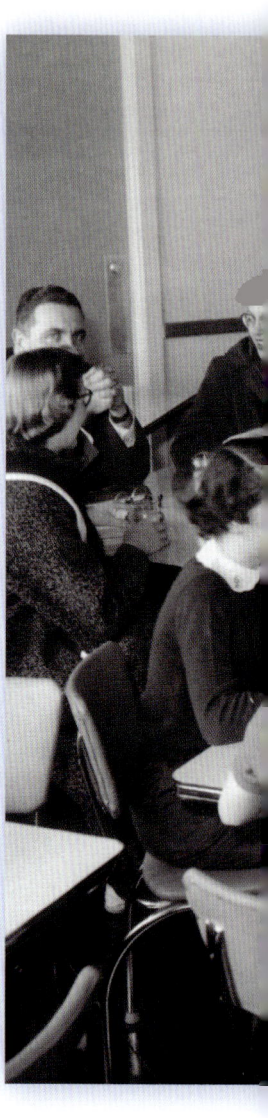

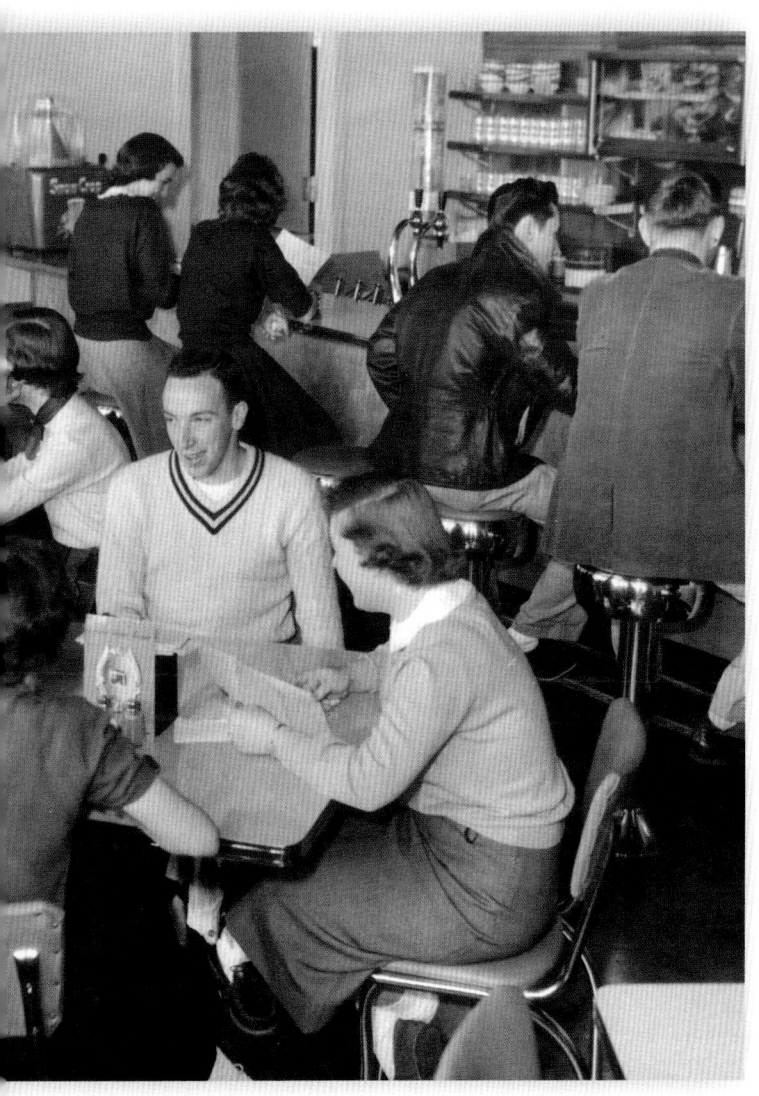

two-straw soda order

Houser's also had a fountain. John's and my favorite from that fountain was a milk shake. Actually, we would have preferred a malted milk, but that cost 25 cents, 5 cents more than a plain milk shake. Our budget allowed us but one milk shake, and so we asked for two straws. The Housers were very understanding and without comment, provided two straws, knowing that when we ordered milk shakes, it was a two-straw order.

Ruth O. Richards

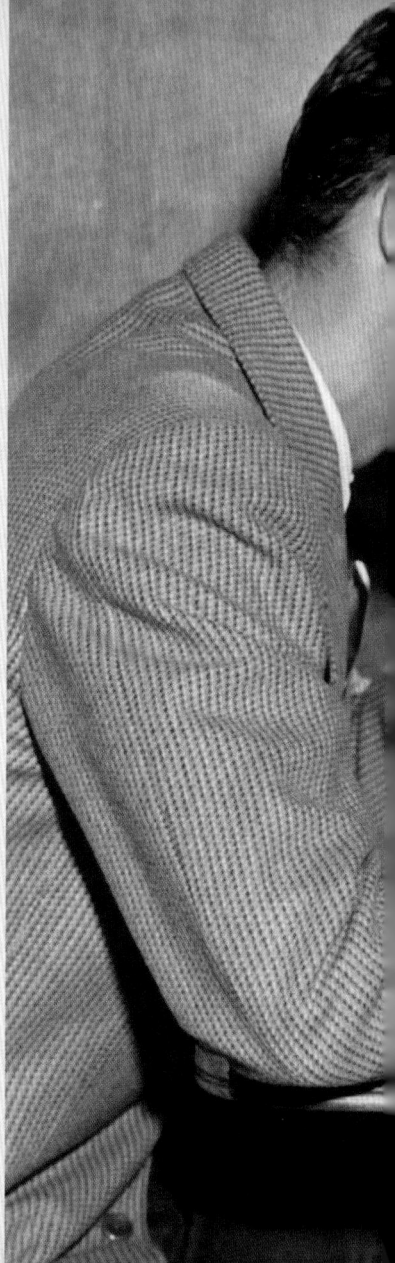

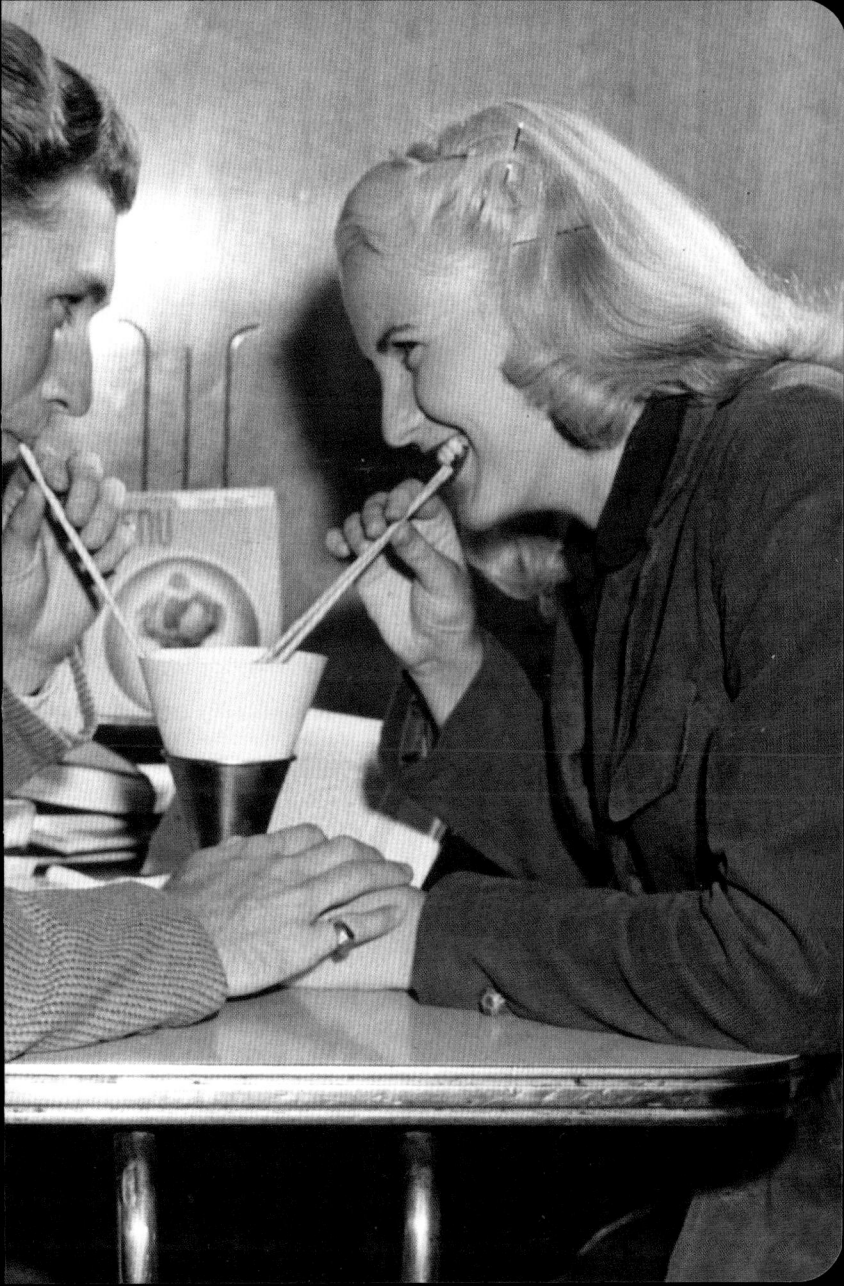

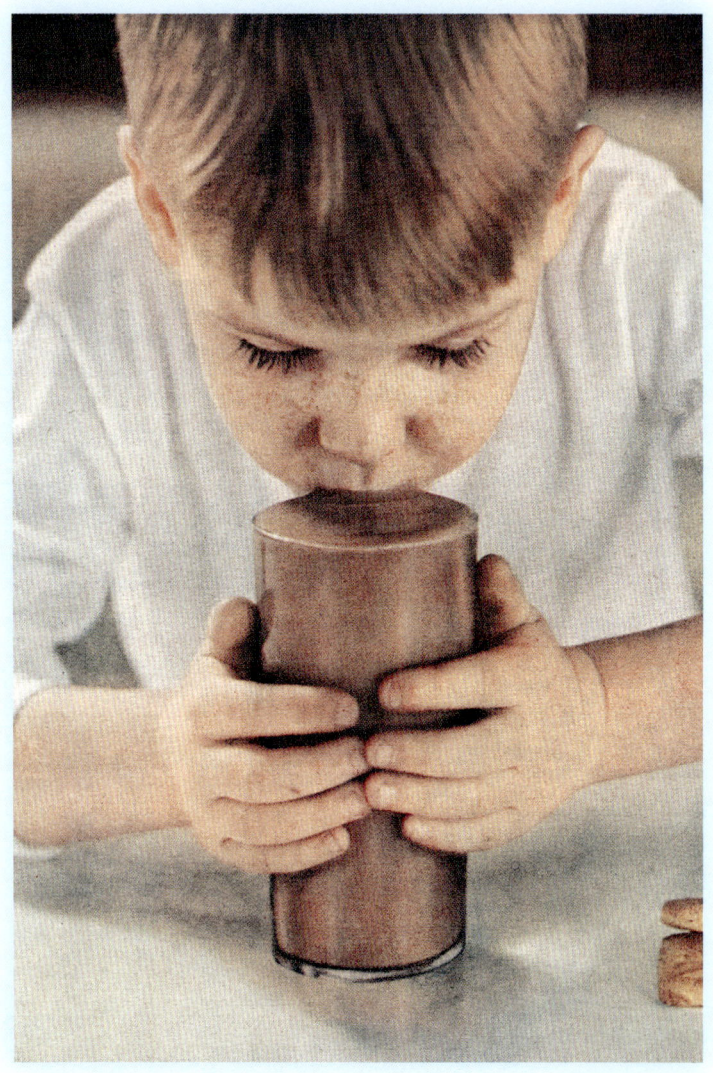

Most of us miss out on life's big prizes. The Pulitzer. The Nobel. Oscars. Emmys. But we're all eligible for life's small pleasures. A pat on the back. A kiss behind the ear. A four-pound bass. A full moon. An empty parking space. A crackling fire. A great meal. A glorious sunset. Hot soup. Cold beer. Don't fret about copping life's grand rewards. Enjoy its tiny delights. There are plenty for all of us.

United Technology Corporation

enjoy the tiny delights

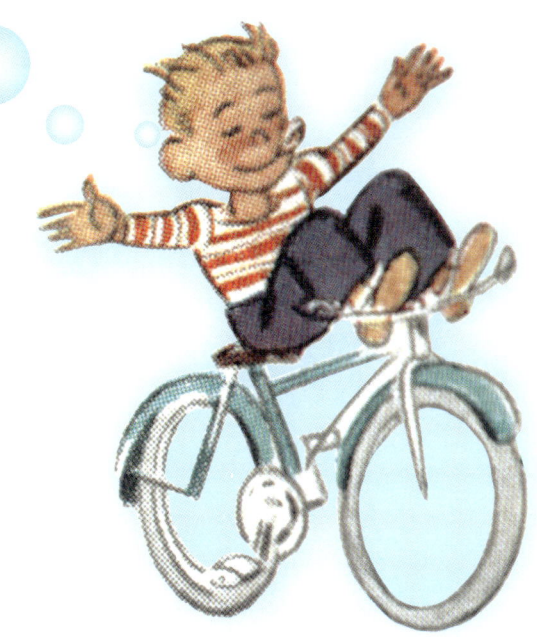

meeting my future wife

She came into the fountain and she was wearing a red dress made out of this special material. She sat down at the fountain and I was polishing the counter. The polish got on the fabric of her dress and made a big hole. It's a wonder she didn't quit me right then!

Kenneth Eck

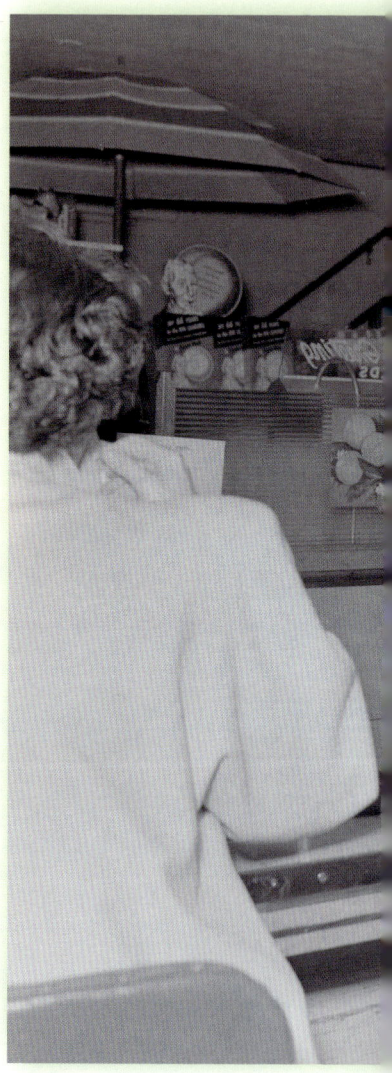

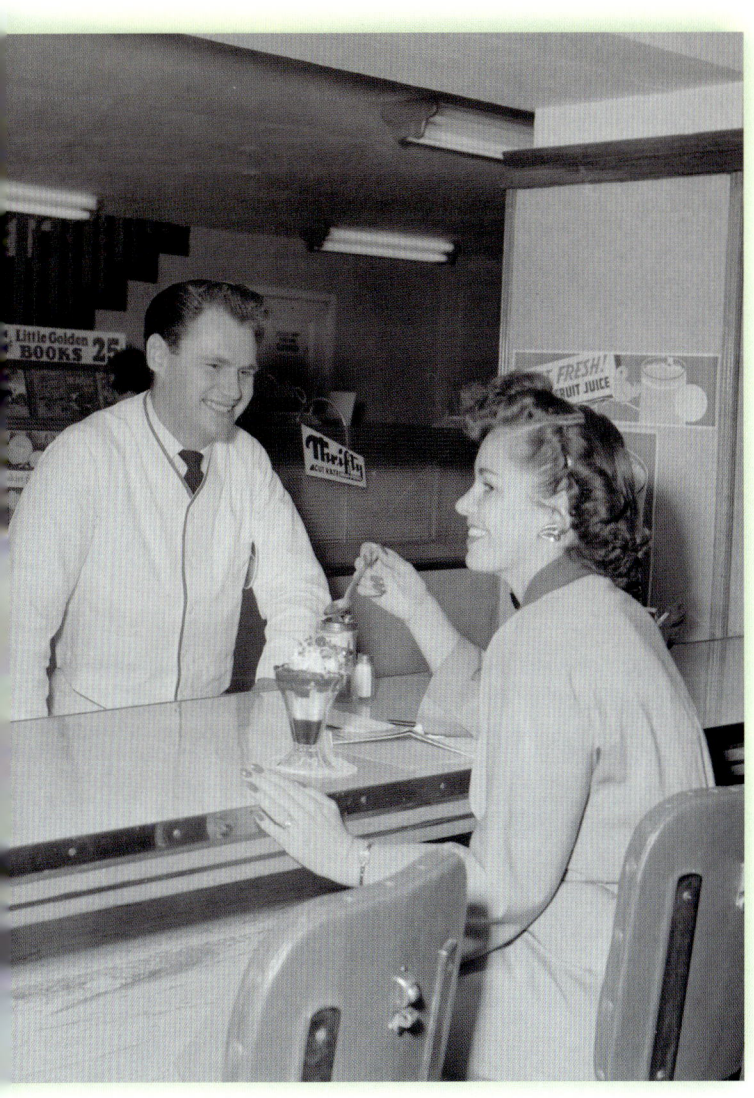

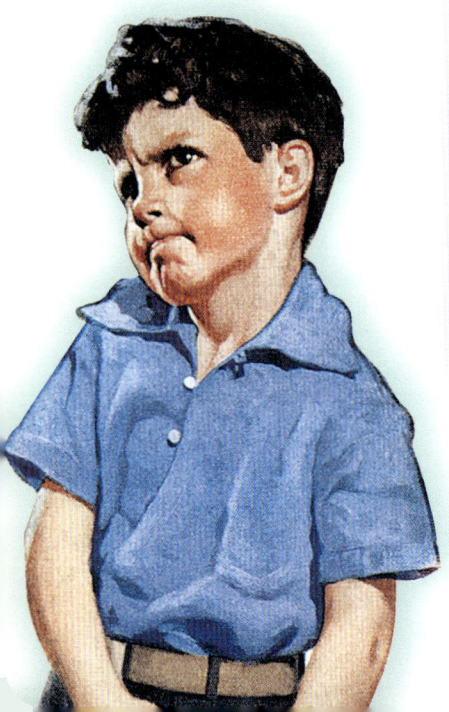
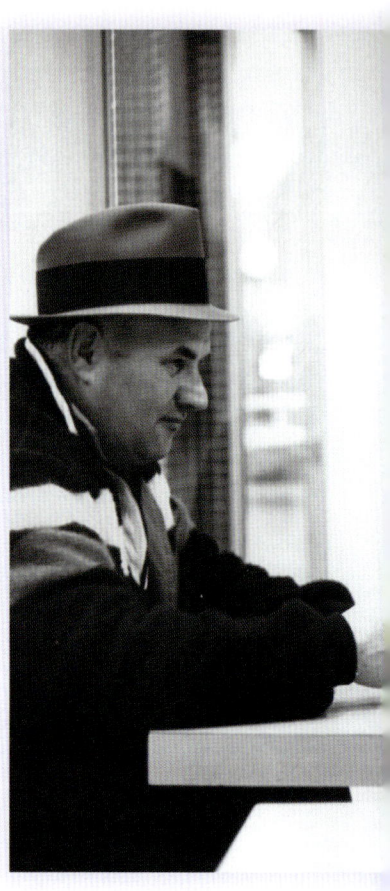

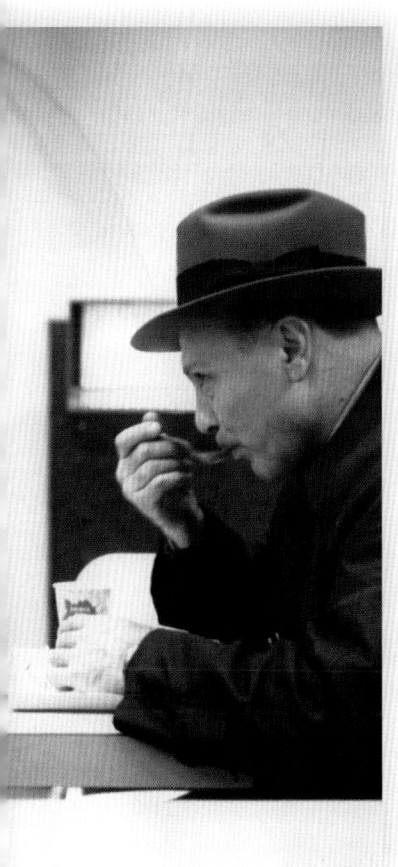

When I delivered a morning paper it was always fun to stop at the Red Cross and listen to Augie and Senator Rasmussen and Clarinda gab in the early morning. I had a way of being semi-invisible around adults so I could eavesdrop. Clarinda cleaned there and had a really loud voice and laughed like a railroad man. Railroad men were tough and ruthless, if not rough and toothless. Anyway it felt like I was in on something I wasn't supposed to be, like secret planning for world domination. Right there in Augie's Red Cross!

Dave Aardappel

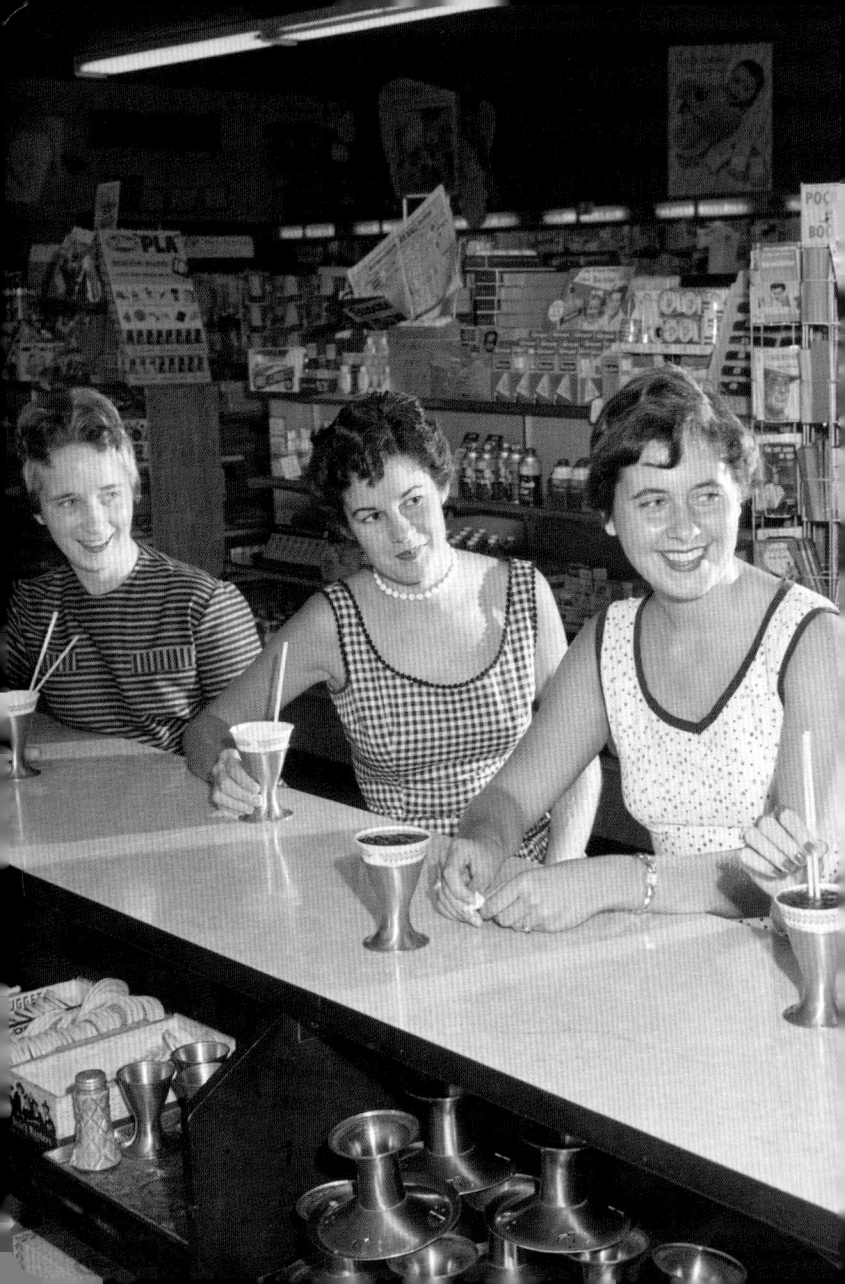

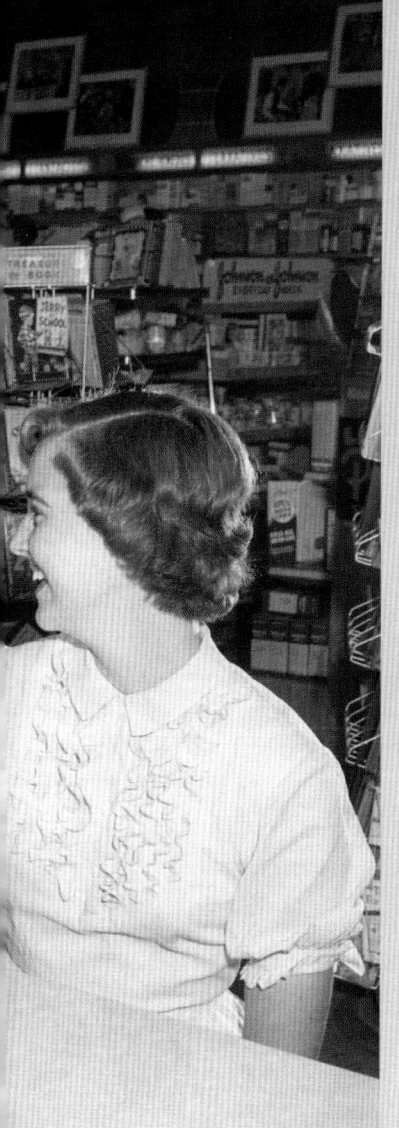

enjoying a little break

The thing I remember most about the 1950s was all the 5-cent drinks I sold (these were drinks made in 6-oz. glasses). Now that size sells for 50 cents! And so many more people came to the soda fountain to socialize. The employees of businesses in town would come down on their breaks for drinks, they didn't have soda machines or anything like that. We used this large old ice grinder to grind the ice—and you always whacked your knuckles when you cranked the handle.

Richard Huckriede

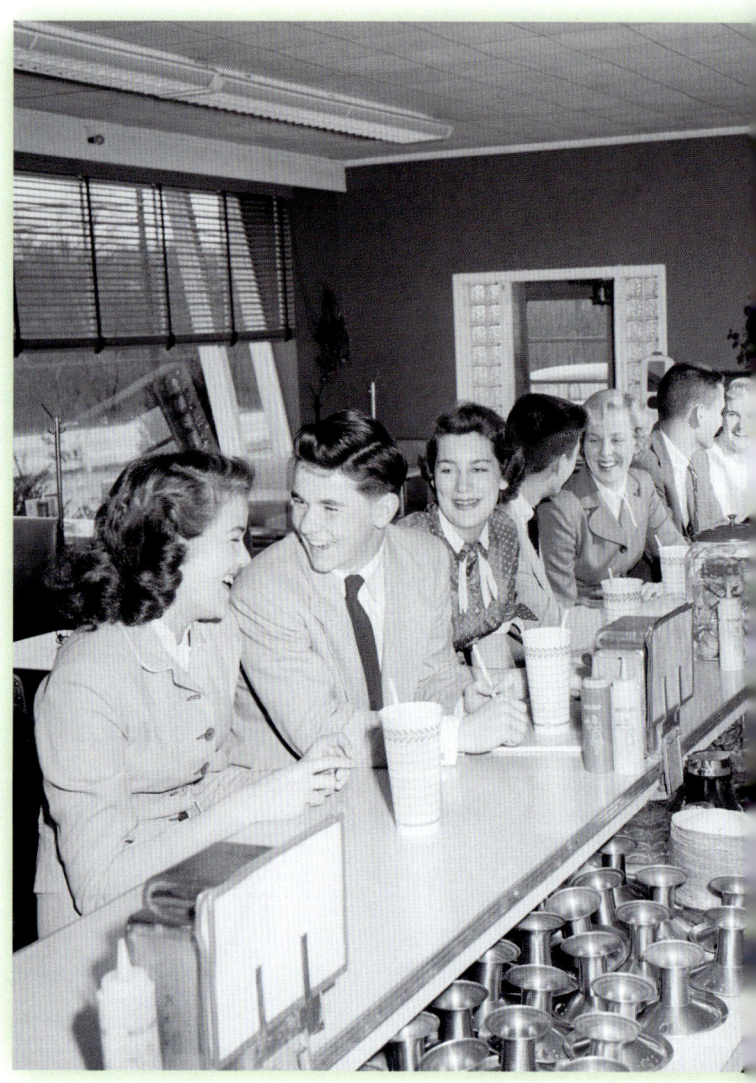

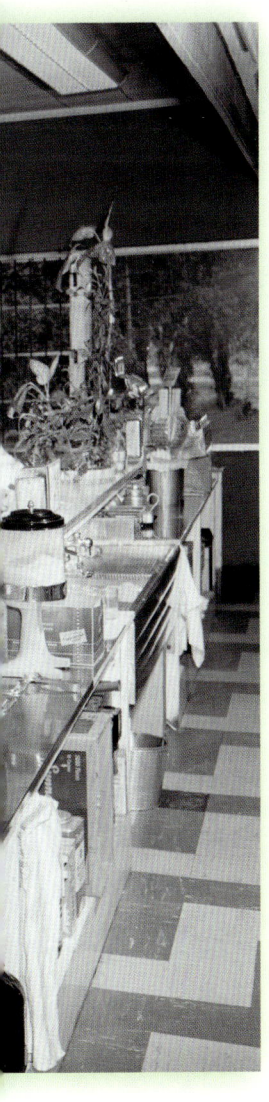

"What really distinguishes ice-cream parlors is their atmosphere and therein lies the difference between a sundae that satisfies the palate and one that satisfies the soul."

Fran R. Schumer

"Some say the glass is half empty, some say the glass is...

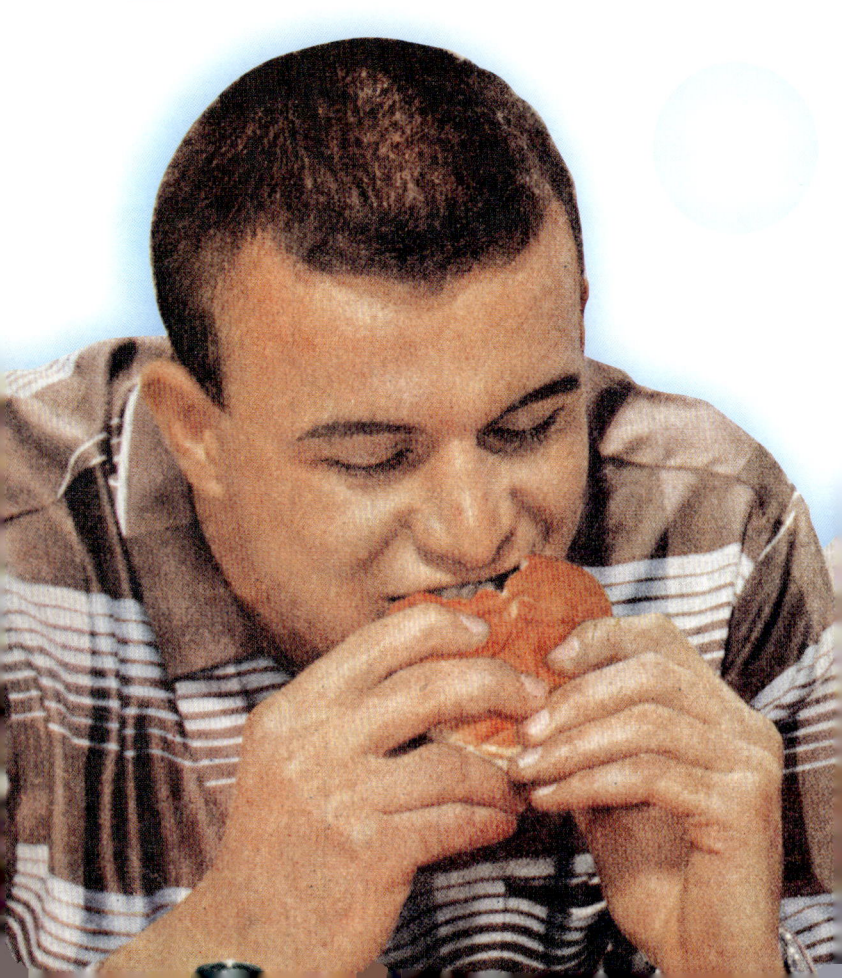

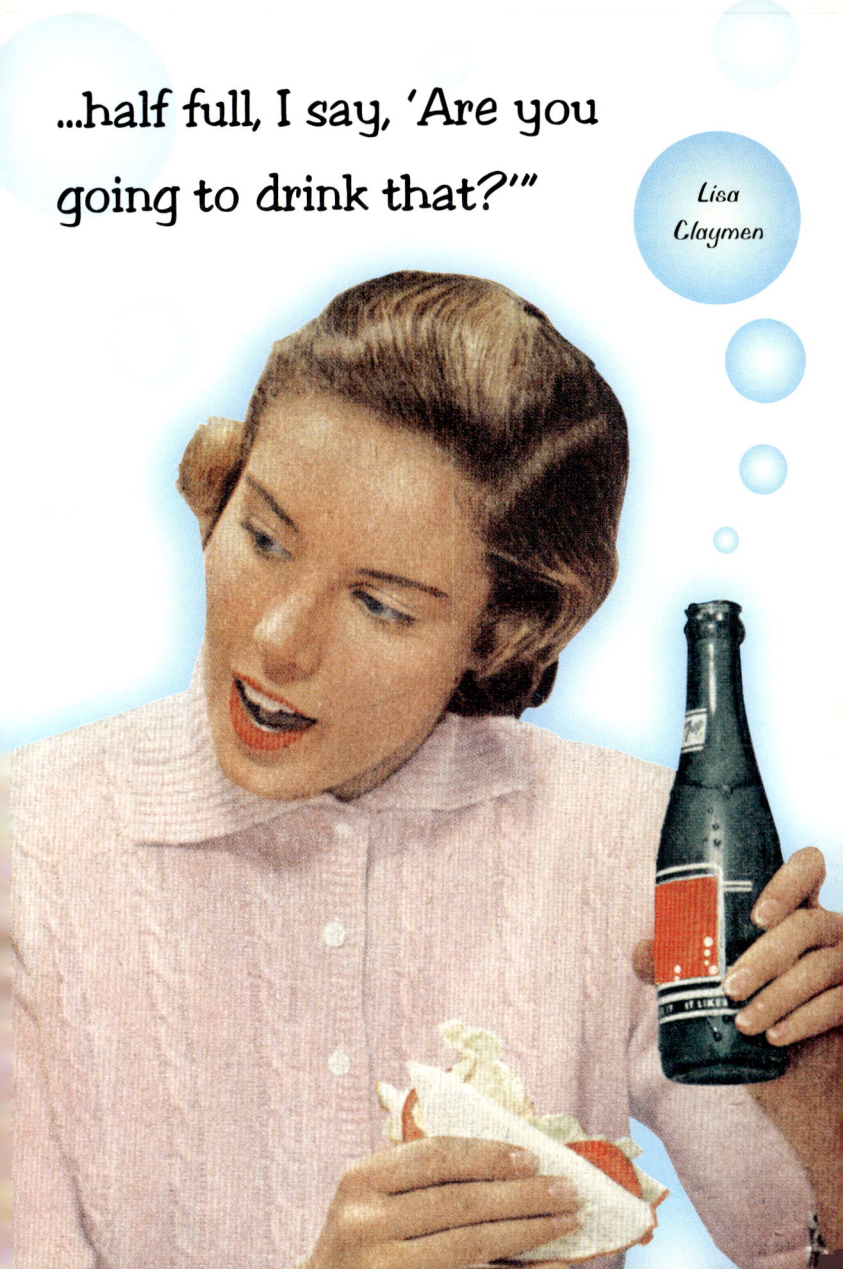

finding Lana Turner

She was "discovered" for movies in the drugstore, sitting at the soda fountain. Thousands of girls have since sat at drugstore fountains drinking sodas and waiting to be discovered. They only got fat from the sodas.

Sidney Skolsky

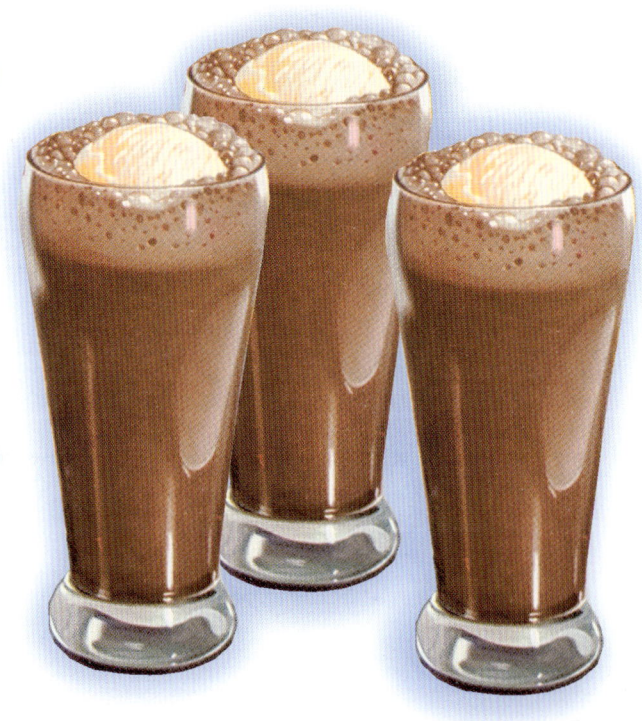

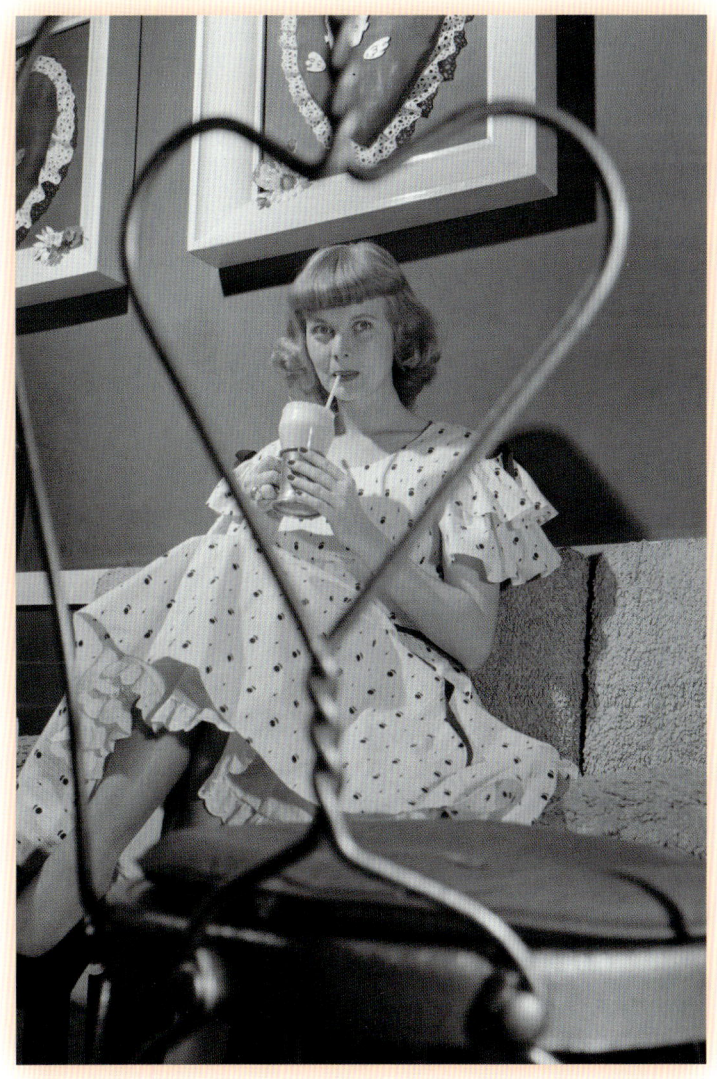

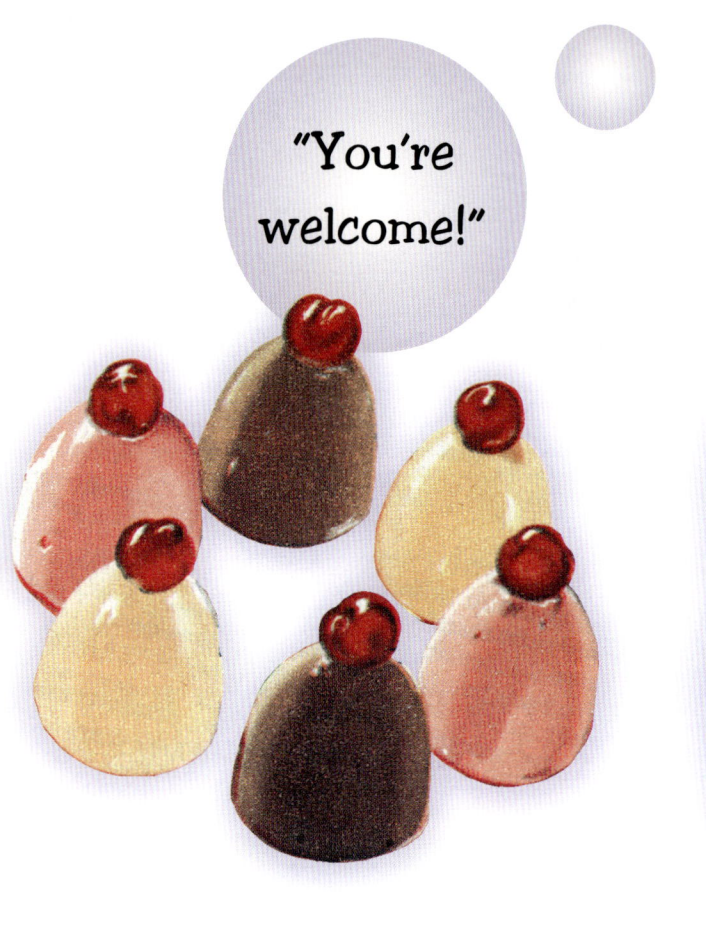

"You're welcome!"

"A little of what you fancy does you good!"

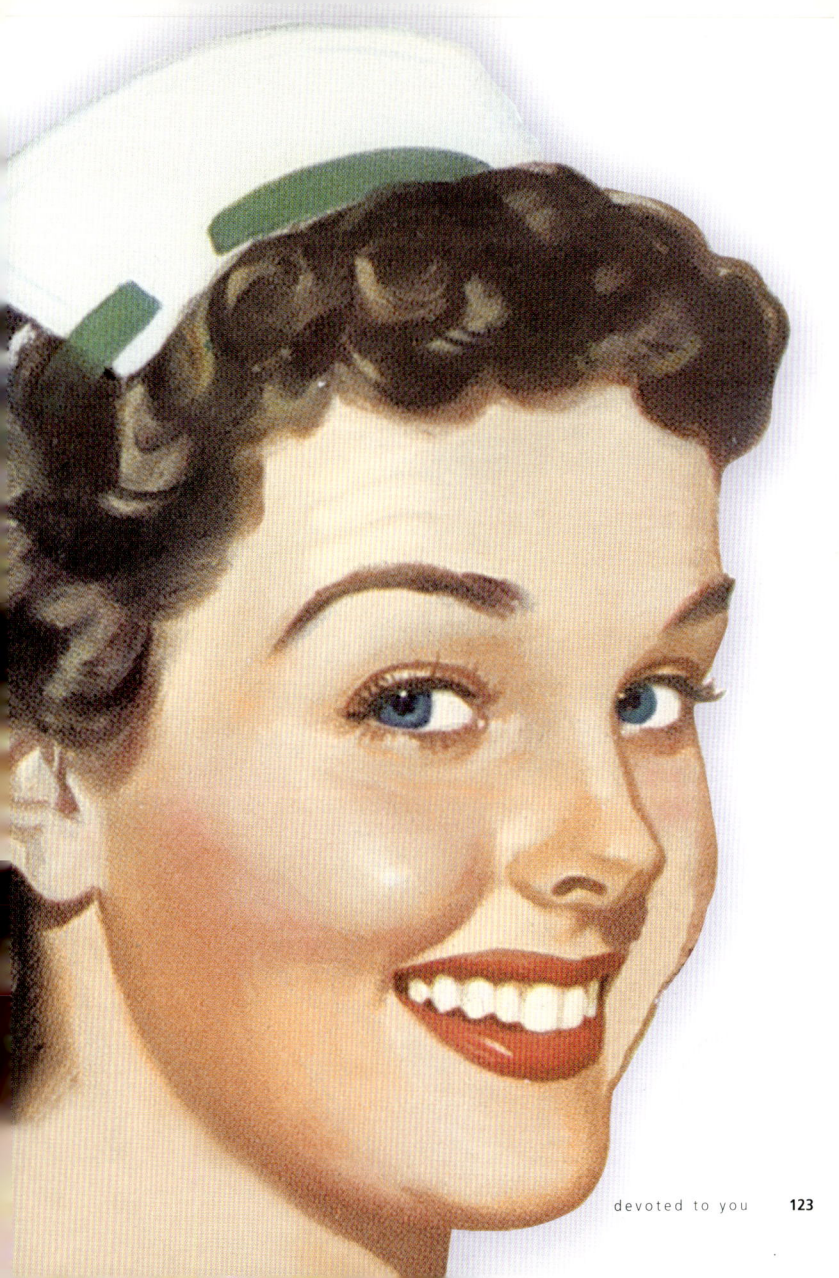

index

A&W 74
Aardappel, Dave 113
advertising 56, 68-9

Bacon, Francis 103
banana split 26, 28, 36, 85
Battleship Sundae 36
Beecher, Henry Ward 95
black-and-white soda 85
Bladen, Thomas 31
bottles, trading in 41
Bromo-Selzer 93
Brooklyn 79
Brooklyn Dodgers 79
Brown, Jaywood Campbell 54
brownies 49
Buffalo Candy Kitchen 12-13, 36
burdock 64

calls 99
candy 16
candy stores 20
"celerystone cola" 67
cherry Coke 43, 72, 85
cherry pie 43
chocolate Coke 72
chocolate ice cream with marshmallow sauce 41
chocolate malt 26
    double 85
    recipe 76-7

chocolate soda 81
chocolate sundaes 25
Christiance, DeForest 35
Christmas 15
City Drug, Wichita Falls 23
Claymen, Lisa 119
Clinton, Jim 95
Coca-Cola 61, 63, 64, 67, 68
commercials 56
Confucius 83
cookies 49

Dairy Queen and King's X 74
dandelion 64
department stores 85
Dervis, Peter 89
dime stores 9, 15, 23
diners 99
double chocolate malt 85
Dowling, Lynne 19
Dr Pepper 64
drugstore cowboys 104
drugstores 9, 11, 19, 89
    being "discovered" in 120
Dunwell, Charlie 49

Eck, Kenneth 90, 110
Edwards, Danny 56
Egg Cream 79
Eliot's drugstore 25, 61
Emerson, Ralph Waldo 28
Emery, Glenn 85
Evans, Will 16

Evanston, Illinois 33

five-and-tens 85
5-cent drinks 115
FIZZicians 90
fizzy drinks 63
flavoring 9, 11, 26
Flippin's 104
folk medicine 64
"fountain professional" 89
fountainers 90
400s 93
fruit drinks 20
fruitcake 49
fudge sauce 50
Fussell, Jacob 31

ginger 64
ginger ale 67
ginger beer 61
groceries 85
grades, good, free soda for 87, 101

Hammond, Laverne 13
Highland, Illinois 72
Hires Root Beer 64
Holt, Miss Edith 104
homemade sweets 49
horseradish 64
hot fudge sundaes 50
Houser's 106
Huckriede, Richard 93, 115
Huntley, Marlene 15

ice cream 28, 54
    etiquette of eating 39
    evening sales 31
    history 31
    passion for 53-8
    University of Kansas cheer 53
ice cream freezer, first 31
ice cream industry 31
ice-cream parlors 117
ice cream sodas, sales forbidden on Sundays 33

James Beard Foundation 63
James, Bebe 43
Jayhawk soda fountain 42
Jefferson, Thomas 31
Johnson, Nancy M. 31

Kansas City, Missouri 19
    University cheer 53
Kenosha, Wisconsin 12-13
Kukla and Ollie 56

language, cryptic 63
Laurence, Don Harold 104
Leacock, Stephen 25, 61
lemon sours 25
lemons 64
lingo 63, 96
Long, Mike 87
luncheonettes 85

Madison, James 31

malted milk 106
Mariposa 25
menu, choices 26
milk shake 106
Miller, Jim 23
Miss Piggy 58
molasses 64
movies, being discovered for 120
Moxie 68-9

New York 79
Newark, New Jersey 31
nutmeg 64

Olney, Judith 50
Owen, Rod 75

Pemberton, John 67
People's Drugstore 41
Pepsi-Cola 64, 67
pharmacies 89
phosphates 11, 19, 61, 63
   fruit-flavored 67
phosphoric acid 63
pineapple sundae 26, 28
   recipe 47
plain 20
Platt, Chester 35
Post, Emily 39
Prussick, Phyllis 20, 79

Rasmussen, Senator 113
Red Cross 113

Reese, Tom 41
refrigeration 85
report cards, free soda for good grades 87, 101
Rexall Drug Store 72, 81
Richards, Babs 81
Richards, Ruth O. 106
root beer 13, 61, 75

St Louis 49
Sandburg, Carl 9
sarsaparilla 25, 64
Schumer, Fran R. 117
Scott, John M. 35
seltzer 20
7-Up 64
Skolsky, Sidney 120
socializing 115
soda fountains 11, 85
   Art-Deco 13
   calls 99
   human dramas in 102
   owners of 82, 87
   waiting to be discovered at 120
   where found 9, 85, 89
soda jerks 63, 82, 85, 89
   alternative names 90
   lingo 63, 96
soda pops 64
soda water 11
sodas 9
   flavors 9, 11, 26
   free offers 100

sodaless 33
two-straw 106
sorrel 64
Stieb, Dan 72
strawberry floats 85
strawberry malt 23
strawberry soda 72
recipe 70-1
sundaes 9
invention 33, 35

temperance movement 61, 67
Thea Soda 67
Truman, Harry S. 95
Turner, Lana 120
tutti-frutti 26, 28
two-straw orders 106

United Technology Corporation 109
University of Kansas cheer 53

vanilla Coke 72
Vernon's Ginger Ale 64

Walgreens, St Louis 49
Ward's Drugs 16
Washington, George 31
White, Joel 101
Wichita Falls 23
Wiemans 15
wife, future, meeting 110
Wilder, Thornton 44
Willard, Frances 33
Wilson, Jeannie 26

Picture credits

CORBIS: 10; 14; 21; 22; 30; 35; 45; 52; 55; 66; 74; 84; 94; 110; 115; 116;119;
GETTY IMAGES: 6 also on p. 80; 12; 17;18; 24; 34; 40; 48; 51; 62; 65; 73; 78; 86; 91; 97; 98; 100; 107; 113; 121
ADVERTISING ARCHIVES: 27
THE KOBAL COLLECTION: 59 MGM/The Kobal Collection

Acknowledgments

9 Excerpt from Carl Sandburg's *Cornhuskers* (New York: Henry Holt & Co. 1918); 12 and 36 Laverne Hammond; 15 Marlene Huntley; 16 Will Evans; 19 Lynne Dowling; 20 and 79 Phyllis Prussick; 23 Jim Miller; 25 and 61 Excerpt from Stephen Leacock's *Sunshine Sketches of a Little Town* John Lane Company, New York; 26 Jeannie Wilson; 28 Excerpt from Ralph Waldo Emerson's 'Man the Reformer' 1841; 33 William Lyon Phelps; 35 Deforest Christiance; 39 Excerpt from *Emily Post's Advice for Every Dining Occasion*, 1922; 41 Tom Reese; 43 Bebe James; 44 Excerpt from Thornton Wilder's "The Skin of Our Teeth" 1942; 49 Charlie Dunwell; 50 Judith Olney; 54 Heywood Campbell Brown; 56 Danny Edwards; 58 Miss Piggy (The Jim Henson Company); 63 The James Beard Foundation; 72 Dan Stieb, The Prairie Moon Company 75 Rod Owen; 81 Babs Richards; 85 Glenn Emery; 87 Mike Long; 89 Peter Dervis; 90 and 110 Kenneth Eck; 93 and 115 Richard Huckriede; 95 Excerpt from Harry S. Truman *Memoirs* 1955-1956, Doubleday, New York; 100 Joel White; 104 Don Harold Lawrence; 106 Ruth O. Richards; 109 United Technologies Corporation Advertisement; 113 Dave Aardappel; 117 Excerpt from Fran R. Schumer's "Flavors of Ice-Cream Parlors: Nostalgic to New" *New York Times* 20 Aug 1986; 118 Lisa Claymen; 120 Sidney Skolsky